Easy Chinese Cookbook

Authentic Asian Food Chinese Style

By
BookSumo Press
All rights reserved

Published by
http://www.booksumo.com

Table of Contents

Chinese Spiced Rice 7

Easiest Dumplings 8

Rhubarb Dumplings 9

Shrimp Soup 10

Spicy Tomato Chicken 11

Chicken Salad 12

Sesame Ramen Coleslaw 13

Natural Ramen Noodles 14

Cabbage Ramen Salad 15

Rice-Noodle Salad 16

A Chicken & Curry Soup 17

Easy Wonton Soup 18

Spicy Beef Spring Rolls 19

Hangzhou Soup 20

Tianjin Province Stir Fry 21

Bok Choy Mushrooms and Chestnuts 22

Suzhou Five Spice Bok Choy 23

North Chinese Style Cabbage 24

Classical Homemade Peking Duck 101 25

Lemon and Garlic Cured Duck 27

Noodles & Shrimp Asian Style 28

Chicken and Onion Egg Noodle Dump Dinner 29

Hearty Chili Noodles Bake 30

Comforting Noodle Soup 31

Tastier Noodles Bake 32

Easy Homemade Noodles 33

Family-Friendly Noodle Casserole 34

Egg Rolls 35

Hot and Spicy Seafood Filets 36

Shrimp Wok 37

Spring Roll Bowls 38

How to Mince Chicken Chinese Style 39

Chicken & Saucy Noodles 40

Vanilla Crusted Shrimp 41

Tofu and Beef Burgers 42

A Uniquely Simple Cumber Soup 43

Maple Wontons 44

Silver Dragon Wonton Soup 45

Cucumber Wontons 46

Artisanal Wonton Tins 47

Cabbage and Shrimp 48

Beef and Lettuce 49

Pierogies Re-Imagined 50

Turkey Bacon Dumplings 51

Meat Kabobs 52

Spicy Eggs 53

Shrimp Veggie Salad 54

Shrimp Spring Rolls 55

Broccoli Ramen Salad 56

Beef Ramen Stir-Fry 57

Ramen for College 58

Sesame Chili Beef 59

Fish Sauce, Garlic Beef 60

Peking Fried Rice 61

Chicken Stir Fry with Noodles 62

Garlicky Bok Choy 63

Bok Choy Skillet 64

Bok Choy Appetizer 65

Tuesday's Bok Choy Long Grain Rice 66

20 Min Vegetarian Bok Choy 67

Gourmet Duck Rice 68

Sunday Night Duck 70

Chinese Styled Duck Rice 71

Homemade Egg Noodles 72

Chinese Noodle Salad 73

Eggy-Weggy Noodle Bake 74

Oyster Sauce Beef Skewers 75

Chicken Pesto 76

Chinese Backyard Chicken Thighs 77

Sweet and Sour Pie 78

Bean Sprouts Egg Rolls 79

Chicken and Jasmine Soup 80

Curried Beef Fillets with Eggplant and Lime 81

Barbecue Bacon Pancakes 82

Grilled Tuna Salad 83

Spicy Lime Shrimp 84

Weeknight Ground Beef Wontons 85

Mozzarella Wonton Bites 86

Wontons Chips with Style 87

How to Make Wonton Wraps 88

Ginger Fish Patties 89

Chinese Spiced Rice

Prep Time: 10 mins
Total Time: 35 mins

Servings per Recipe: 8
Calories   226 kcal
Carbohydrates   39.8 g
Cholesterol   0 mg
Fat   5.5 g
Protein   3.7 g
Sodium   4 mg

Ingredients

- 3 tbsps vegetable oil
- 1 large onion, chopped
- 2 jalapeno peppers, seeded and minced
- 2 cloves garlic, crushed
- 1 tsp ground turmeric
- 1/2 tsp ground cinnamon
- 2 cups uncooked long-grain white rice
- 2 (14.5 ounce) cans chicken broth
- 1 cup water
- 1 bay leaf
- 2 green onions, chopped

Directions

1. Cook onion, garlic and jalapeno peppers for about eight minutes before adding turmeric and cooking for two more minutes.
2. Now add chicken broth, bay leaf and water, and cook all this for about 20 minutes after bringing this mixture to boil.
3. Turn the heat off and let it stand as it is for about five minutes.
4. Sprinkle some green onion over it before serving.

EASIEST Dumplings

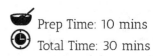
Prep Time: 10 mins
Total Time: 30 mins

Servings per Recipe: 12
Calories	186 kcal
Carbohydrates	25.7 g
Cholesterol	2 mg
Fat	7.3 g
Protein	4.2 g
Sodium	466 mg

Ingredients

1 1/2 cups all-purpose flour
2 tsps baking powder
3/4 tsp salt
3 tbsps shortening

3/4 cup milk

Directions

1. Mix flour, salt and baking powder in a bowl before adding shortening into it and whisking it thoroughly.
2. Now add some milk to get it moist.
3. Now put dumplings by the spoonful into any boiling stew or soup and cook it for 10 minutes uncovered and then another 10 minutes covered.
4. Serve.

Rhubarb Dumplings

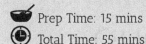

Prep Time: 15 mins
Total Time: 55 mins

Servings per Recipe: 10
Calories   275 kcal
Carbohydrates   36 g
Cholesterol   25 mg
Fat   13.9 g
Protein   2.6 g
Sodium   408 mg

Ingredients

1 (12 ounce) can refrigerated buttermilk biscuit dough
2 cups chopped fresh rhubarb
1 cup white sugar
1 cup water
1/2 cup butter, melted
1 1/4 tsps vanilla extract
1/4 tsp ground cinnamon, or to taste

Directions

1. Set your oven to 350 degrees F before doing anything else.
2. Make 3 inch circles from the biscuits and then fold it around rhubarb placed at its center.
3. Now place these dumplings in a baking dish and then pour a mixture of sugar, vanilla, water and butter over it before sprinkling some cinnamon.
4. Now bake this for about 40 minutes in a preheated oven or until you see that the biscuits are golden brown.

SHRIMP Soup

Prep Time: 15 mins
Total Time: 40 mins

Servings per Recipe: 6
Calories   212 kcal
Carbohydrates   28.6 g
Cholesterol   52 mg
Fat   4.7 g
Protein   14.4 g
Sodium   1156 mg

Ingredients

1 tbsp vegetable oil
2 tsps minced fresh garlic
2 tsps minced fresh ginger root
1 (10 ounce) package frozen chopped spinach, thawed and drained
salt and black pepper to taste
2 quarts chicken stock
1 cup shrimp stock
1 tsp hot pepper sauce(optional)
1 tsp hoisin sauce(optional)
20 peeled and deveined medium shrimp
1 (6.75 ounce) package long rice noodles (rice vermicelli)
2 green onions, chopped(optional)

Directions

1. Cook garlic and ginger for about one minute before adding spinach, pepper and salt, and cooking it for 3 more minutes to get the spinach tender.
2. Add chicken stock, hoisin sauce, shrimp stock and hot pepper sauce, and cook this for a few more minutes.
3. In the end, add noodles and shrimp into it, and cook it for 4 minutes before adding green onions cooking it for another five minutes.
4. Add salt and pepper according to your taste before serving.
5. Enjoy.

Spicy Tomato Chicken

Prep Time: 20 mins
Total Time: 55 mins

Servings per Recipe: 4
Calories	462 kcal
Carbohydrates	15.4 g
Cholesterol	92 mg
Fat	29.7 g
Protein	33.6 g
Sodium	183 mg

Ingredients

1 (3 pound) whole chicken, cut into 8 pieces
1 tsp ground turmeric
salt to taste
1/4 cup dried red chili peppers
3 fresh red chili pepper, finely chopped
4 cloves garlic, minced
1 red onion, chopped
1 (3/4 inch thick) slice fresh ginger root
2 tbsps sunflower seed oil
1 cinnamon stick
2 whole star anise pods
5 whole cloves
5 cardamom seeds
2 tomatoes, sliced
2 tbsps ketchup
1 tsp white sugar, or to taste
1/2 cup water

Directions

1. Coat chicken with turmeric powder and salt, and set it aside for later use.
2. Put dried red chili peppers in hot water until you see that it is soft.
3. Put softened dried chili, garlic, fresh red chili peppers, onion, and ginger in a blender and blend it until you get a paste.
4. Cook chicken in hot oil until you see that it is golden from all sides and set it aside.
5. Now cook chili paste, cinnamon, cardamom seeds, star anise, and cloves in the same pan for few minutes before adding chicken and water into it.
6. Add tomatoes, sugar and ketchup, and bring all this to a boil before turning down the heat to medium and cooking for another 15 minutes.
7. Serve.

CHICKEN Salad

🥣 Prep Time: 30 mins
🕐 Total Time: 30 mins

Servings per Recipe: 4
Calories   303 kcal
Carbohydrates   19.3 g
Cholesterol   37 mg
Fat   17.9 g
Protein   19.2 g
Sodium   991 mg

Ingredients

1 tbsp finely chopped green chile peppers
1 tbsp rice vinegar
2 tbsps fresh lime juice
3 tbsps Asian fish sauce
3 cloves garlic, minced
1 tbsp white sugar
1 tbsp Asian (toasted) sesame oil
2 tbsps vegetable oil
1 tsp black pepper
2 cooked skinless boneless chicken breast halves, shredded
1/2 head cabbage, cored and thinly sliced
1 carrot, cut into matchsticks
1/3 onion, finely chopped
1/3 cup chopped fresh cilantro

Directions

1. Combine chopped green chilies, sesame oil, lime juice, fish sauce, garlic, sugar, rice vinegar, vegetable oil and black pepper in a medium sized bowl very thoroughly so that the sugar is completely dissolved.
2. Mix chicken, carrot, onion, cabbage and cilantro in a separate bowl.
3. Pour the bowl containing dressing over this and serve it after thoroughly mixing it.

Sesame Ramen Coleslaw

Prep Time: 15 mins
Total Time: 25 mins

Servings per Recipe: 4
Calories   253 kcal
Carbohydrates   30.5 g
Cholesterol   0 mg
Fat   12.5 g
Protein   7.1 g
Sodium   543 mg

Ingredients

2 tbsps vegetable oil
3 tbsps white vinegar
2 tbsps white sugar
1 (3 ounce) package chicken flavored ramen noodles, crushed, seasoning packet reserved
1/2 tsp salt
1/2 tsp ground black pepper
2 tbsps sesame seeds
1/4 cup sliced almonds
1/2 medium head cabbage, shredded
5 green onions, chopped

Directions

1. Set your oven at 350 degrees F and also put some oil on the baking dish.
2. Mix oil, ramen noodle mix, salt, vinegar, pepper and sugar in a bowl to be used as a dressing.
3. Bake sesame seeds and almonds in the preheated oven for about 10 minutes.
4. Coat the mixture of cabbage, crushed ramen noodles and greens onions with the dressing very thoroughly before topping it with sesame seeds and almonds.
5. Serve.

NATURAL
Ramen Noodles

🥣 Prep Time: 10 mins
⏲ Total Time: 20 mins

Servings per Recipe: 4
Calories   280 kcal
Carbohydrates   53.6 g
Cholesterol   0 mg
Fat   4.4 g
Protein   10.4 g
Sodium   1351 mg

Ingredients

4 cups vegetable broth
4 cups water
1 tbsp soy sauce
1 tbsp sesame oil
1 tbsp ground ginger

1 tbsp Sriracha hot sauce
9 ounces soba noodles

Directions

1. Bring everything except noodles to boil before adding noodles and cooking it for about seven minutes or until you see that they are tender.
2. Take noodles out into bowls and top with broth according to your choice.

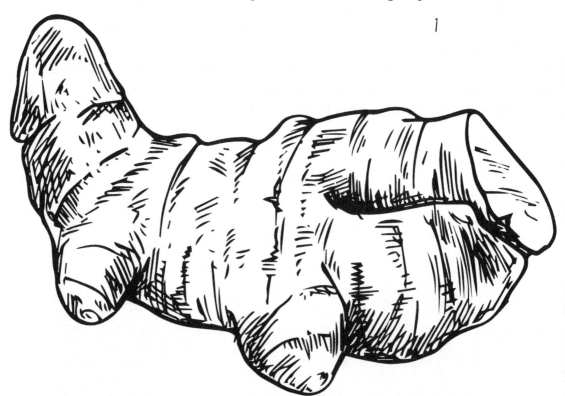

Cabbage Ramen Salad

Prep Time: 15 mins
Total Time: 25 mins

Servings per Recipe: 6
Calories   266 kcal
Carbohydrates   16.2 g
Cholesterol   < 1 mg
Fat   22.6 g
Protein   1.8 g
Sodium   82 mg

Ingredients

1/2 large head cabbage, coarsely chopped
1 (3 ounce) package ramen noodles, crushed
1/2 cup sunflower seeds
1/2 cup vegetable oil
3 tbsps white sugar
3 tbsps distilled white vinegar

Directions

1. Pour a mixture of vinegar, ramen flavor packet, sugar and oil over the mixture of cabbage, sunflower seeds and noodles.
2. Mix it very thoroughly before serving.

RICE-NOODLE
Salad

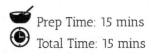
Prep Time: 15 mins
Total Time: 15 mins

Servings per Recipe: 4
Calories   432 kcal
Carbohydrates   89.5 g
Cholesterol   0 mg
Fat   5.3 g
Protein   6.6 g
Sodium   188 mg

Ingredients

5 cloves garlic
1 cup loosely packed chopped cilantro
1/2 jalapeno pepper, seeded and minced
3 tbsps white sugar
1/4 cup fresh lime juice
3 tbsps vegetarian fish sauce
1 (12 ounce) package dried rice noodles
2 carrots, julienned
1 cucumber, halved lengthwise and chopped
1/4 cup chopped fresh mint
4 leaves napa cabbage
1/4 cup unsalted peanuts
4 sprigs fresh mint

Directions

1. Add a mashed mixture of hot pepper, garlic and cilantro into the bowl containing mixture of lime juice, sugar and fish sauce before letting it stand for at least five minutes.
2. Cook rice noodles in boiling salty water for two minutes before draining it and passing it through cold water to stop the process of cooking.
3. Mix sauce, carrots, cucumber, noodles, mint and Napa in large sized serving bowl very thoroughly before garnishing it with peanuts and mint sprigs.

A Chicken & Curry Soup

🥣 Prep Time: 30 mins
🕐 Total Time: 2 hrs 30 mins

Servings per Recipe: 8
Calories	512 kcal
Carbohydrates	40.6 g
Cholesterol	75 mg
Fat	26.8 g
Protein	29.8 g
Sodium	374 mg

Ingredients

- 2 tbsps vegetable oil
- 1 (3 pound) whole chicken, skin removed and cut into pieces
- 1 onion, cut into chunks
- 2 shallots, thinly sliced
- 2 cloves garlic, chopped
- 1/8 cup thinly sliced fresh ginger root
- 1 stalk lemon grass, cut into 2 inch pieces
- 4 tbsps curry powder
- 1 green bell pepper, cut into 1 inch pieces
- 2 carrots, sliced diagonally
- 1 quart chicken broth
- 1 quart water
- 2 tbsps fish sauce
- 2 kaffir lime leaves
- 1 bay leaf
- 2 tsps red pepper flakes
- 8 small potatoes, quartered
- 1 (14 ounce) can coconut milk
- 1 bunch fresh cilantro

Directions

1. Cook onion and chicken in hot oil until you see that onions are soft and then set it aside for later use.
2. Cook shallots in the same pan for one minute before adding garlic, lemon grass, ginger and curry powder, and cooking it for another five minutes.
3. Add pepper and carrots before stirring in chicken, onion, fish sauce, chicken broth and water.
4. Also add lime leaves, red pepper flakes and bay leaf before bringing all this to boil and adding potatoes.
5. Add coconut milk and cook it for 60 minutes after turning down the heat to low.
6. Garnish with a sprig of fresh cilantro.
7. Serve.

EASY
Wonton Soup

🍲 Prep Time: 5 mins
🕐 Total Time: 15 mins

Servings per Recipe: 4
Calories   293 kcal
Fat   9 g
Carbohydrates   33.5g
Protein   17.7 g
Cholesterol   84 mg
Sodium   3373 mg

Ingredients

8 C. chicken broth
3 tbsps soy sauce
2 tsps sesame oil
2 tsps apple juice
2 tsps lemon juice
2 tsps minced garlic

1 1/2 tsps chile-garlic sauce (such as Sriracha(R))
salt to taste
8 C. water
20 wontons

Directions

1. Get the following simmering: salt, broth, chili garlic sauce, sesame oil, garlic, apple juice, and lemon juice.
2. Let the mix gently simmer for 12 mins.
3. At the same time being to get some water boiling in another pot. Add the wontons to the boiling water and let the mix cook for 7 mins. Then combine the wontons to the simmering mix.
4. Enjoy.

Spicy Beef Spring Rolls

Prep Time: 5 mins
Total Time: 15 mins

Servings per Recipe: 20
Calories   177.9
Cholesterol   16.5mg
Sodium   401.6mg
Carbohydrates   15.9g
Protein   7.7g

Ingredients

- 2 tbsps olive oil
- 1 medium onion, chopped
- 1 lb lean ground beef
- 1 tbsp fresh ginger, minced
- 3 garlic cloves, minced
- 1 tsp chili paste
- 1/4 C. soy sauce
- Salt and freshly ground black pepper, to taste
- 1 head green cabbage, cored and shredded
- 2 medium carrots, peeled and grated
- 3 scallions, slice thinly
- 1 tbsp fresh lime juice
- 1 (14-oz.) package spring roll wrappers
- 1/2 C. oil

Directions

1. In a large skillet, heat olive oil and sauté onion till tender.
2. Add beef and cook for about 1-2 minutes.
3. Add ginger, garlic, chili paste, soy sauce, salt and black pepper and cook for about 10-15 minutes.
4. Add cabbage and cook for about 5-10 minutes.
5. Stir in the carrots and stir fry till all the liquid is absorbed.
6. Stir in the scallion and lemon juice and stir fry for about 1 minute and Remove everything from the heat to cool.
7. Place the wrappers onto a smooth surface.
8. Divide the beef mixture in the center of each wrapper evenly.
9. Roll the wrappers around the filling and with your wet fingers brush the edges and press to seal completely.
10. In a large cast-iron skillet, heat the oil.
11. Carefully, add the rolls to the skillet in batches.
12. Fry the rolls till golden brown and transfer onto paper towel lined plates to drain.

HANGZHOU Soup

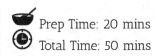

Prep Time: 20 mins
Total Time: 50 mins

Servings per Recipe: 8
Calories	175 kcal
Fat	2.8 g
Carbohydrates	28.8g
Protein	9.6 g
Cholesterol	15 mg
Sodium	470 mg

Ingredients

- 1 tbsp vegetable oil
- 1 yellow onion, diced
- 2 cloves garlic, minced
- 6 C. water
- 4 tsp chicken soup base (such as Better than Bouillon(R))
- 6 small potatoes, diced
- 4 carrots, sliced
- 6 large bok choy ribs with leaves, finely chopped
- 2 stalks celery, sliced
- 2 skinless, boneless chicken breast halves, cut into 1/2-inch cubes

Directions

1. In a large pan, heat the oil on medium heat and sauté the onion and garlic for about 10 minutes.
2. Add the water, chicken base, potatoes, carrots, bok choy and celery and bring to a boil.
3. Reduce the heat and simmer for about 10 minutes.
4. Add chicken and simmer for about 10 minutes.

Tianjin Province Stir Fry

Prep Time: 15 mins
Total Time: 25 mins

Servings per Recipe: 2
Calories   103 kcal
Fat   6.1 g
Carbohydrates   10.7 g
Protein   2.9 g
Cholesterol   15 mg
Sodium   153 mg

Ingredients

- 1 tbsp butter
- 1 small beet, peeled and thinly sliced
- 3 oz. carrots, peeled and thinly sliced
- 3 1/2 oz. daikon radishes, thinly sliced
- 2 Crimini mushrooms, thinly sliced
- 3 1/2 oz. bok choy
- 1/4 tsp ground cardamom

Directions

1. In a skillet, melt the butter on medium-high heat and sauté the beet, carrots, daikon radishes and mushrooms for about 5 minutes.
2. Cover the skillet.
3. Cut the bottom half off bok choy and chop.
4. Slice the bok choy leaves into ribbons.
5. Add the chopped bok choy into the skillet and cook for about 5 minutes.
6. Stir in the cardamom and bok choy leaves and cook for about 1 minute more.

BOK CHOY
Mushrooms and Chestnuts

Prep Time: 20 mins
Total Time: 30 mins

Servings per Recipe: 4
Calories 392 kcal
Fat 16.2 g
Carbohydrates 22.7g
Protein 39.4 g
Cholesterol 113 mg
Sodium 1059 mg

Ingredients

3 squares Land O'Lakes(R) Teriyaki Sauté Express(R)
1 (14 oz.) package chicken breast tenders, cut into bite-sized pieces
1 C. snow peas, trimmed, cut in half
1/2 C. sliced onion
1 (15 oz.) can whole straw mushrooms, drained
1 (8 oz.) can sliced water chestnuts, drained
3 C. sliced bok choy

Directions

1. In a 12-inch nonstick skillet, melt 2 Sauté Express(R) squares on medium heat and cook the chicken for about 5 minutes.
2. Transfer the chicken into a bowl and keep warm.
3. In the same skillet, melt the remaining Sauté Express(R) square on medium heat and cook the snow peas, onion, mushrooms and water chestnuts for about 2-3 minutes.
4. Add the bok choy and cook for about 3-5 minutes.
5. Add the chicken and gently, toss to combine.

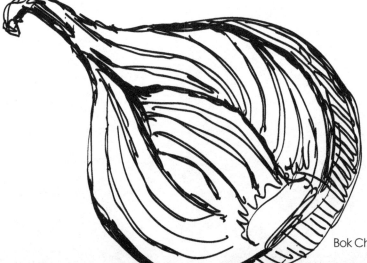

Suzhou Five Spice Bok Choy

Prep Time: 15 mins
Total Time: 25 mins

Servings per Recipe: 4
Calories   164 kcal
Fat   11.9 g
Carbohydrates   12.8g
Protein   4.3 g
Cholesterol   8 mg
Sodium   99 mg

Ingredients

1 large head bok choy
1 tbsp grapeseed oil
1 tbsp butter
1 onion, sliced
1/3 C. cashews
3 cloves garlic, minced
1/2 tsp Chinese five-spice powder
1 pinch white sugar

Directions

1. Cut the root-end of bok choy into 1/2-1-inch slices and discard the stems.
2. Cut the stalks diagonally into 1/8-inch pieces and tear the leaves into bite-sized pieces.
3. In a skillet, heat the oil and butter on medium heat and sauté the onion, cashews, garlic, bok choy, Chinese five-spice and sugar for about 8 to 10 minutes.

NORTH CHINESE STYLE
Cabbage

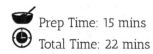

Prep Time: 15 mins
Total Time: 22 mins

Servings per Recipe: 2
Calories   317 kcal
Fat   27.5 g
Carbohydrates   17.9 g
Protein   1.8 g
Cholesterol   0 mg
Sodium   270 mg

Ingredients

1 1/2 tbsp white sugar
1 tbsp brown rice vinegar
1 1/2 tbsp cornstarch
3 tbsp cold water
1/4 C. vegetable oil
3 dried red chili peppers, seeded and thinly sliced
1/2 lb. baby bok choy, trimmed and chopped
salt to taste

Directions

1. In a bowl, mix together the sugar, brown rice vinegar, cornstarch and cold water.
2. In a large skillet, heat the oil on high heat and sauté the chili peppers for about 4 minutes.
3. With a slotted spoon, transfer the chili peppers into a bowl.
4. Add the bok choy and cook for about 1-2 minutes.
5. Add the vinegar sauce and bring to a boil.
6. Cook for about 30 seconds.
7. Remove from the heat and season with the salt.

Classical Homemade Peking Duck 101

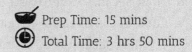

Prep Time: 15 mins
Total Time: 3 hrs 50 mins

Servings per Recipe: 4	
Calories	556 kcal
Fat	31 g
Carbohydrates	48.1g
Protein	22.4 g
Cholesterol	91 mg
Sodium	748 mg

Ingredients

- 1 (4 lb.) whole duck, dressed
- 1/2 tsp ground cinnamon
- 1/2 tsp ground ginger
- 1/4 tsp ground allspice
- 1/4 tsp ground white pepper
- 1/8 tsp ground cloves
- 3 tbsp soy sauce
- 1 tbsp honey
- 1 orange, sliced in rounds
- 1 tbsp chopped fresh parsley, for garnish
- 5 green onions
- 1/2 C. plum jam
- 1 1/2 tsp sugar
- 1 1/2 tsp distilled white vinegar
- 1/4 C. finely chopped chutney

Directions

1. Rinse the duck completely and pat dry.
2. Remove the tail.
3. In a small bowl, mix the cinnamon, ginger, allspice, white pepper and cloves.
4. Season the cavity of the duck with 1 tsp of the ginger mixture.
5. Add 1 tbsp of the soy sauce into the remaining ginger mixture and mix well.
6. Rub the ginger mixture over the duck evenly.
7. Cut one of the green onions in half and tuck inside the cavity.
8. Refrigerate, covered for at least 2 hours or overnight.
9. Set your oven to 375 degrees F.
10. Place duck breast side up on a rack, arranged in a large pan and steam for an hour adding a little more water.
11. With two large spoons, lift the duck and drain the juices and green onion.
12. Place the duck, breast side up in a roasting pan and with a fork, prick the skin all over.
13. Cook in the oven for about 30 minutes.
14. Meanwhile in a bowl, mix together the remaining 2 tbsp of the soy sauce and honey.

15. After 30 minutes, coat the duck with the honey mixture evenly.
16. Now, set the oven to 500 degrees F.
17. Cook in the oven for about 5 minutes.
18. For the sauce in a bowl, mix the plum jam with, sugar, vinegar and chutney.
19. In another bowl, place the remaining chopped green onions.
20. Place whole duck onto a serving platter and garnish with orange slices and fresh parsley.
21. Serve alongside the plum sauce and green onions.

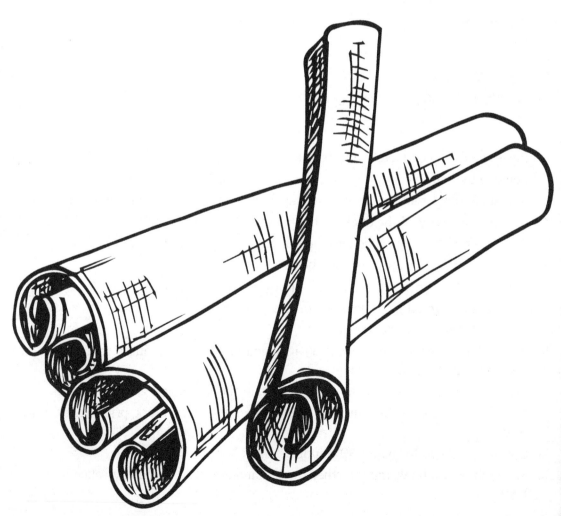

Lemon and Garlic Cured Duck

Prep Time: 30 mins
Total Time: 2 months

Servings per Recipe: 2
Calories   2500 kcal
Fat   270 g
Carbohydrates   9.5g
Protein   20.1 g
Cholesterol   330 mg
Sodium   2989 mg

Ingredients

- 2 uncooked Peking duck legs
- 1 tbsp kosher salt
- 1 lemon, zested and thinly sliced
- 3 cloves garlic, crushed
- 1 tbsp whole allspice berries
- 1 tbsp juniper berries
- 2 sprigs fresh thyme
- 2 C. rendered duck fat

Directions

1. Season the duck legs with the kosher salt evenly.
2. In a large resealable bag, place the duck legs with the lemon zest and slices, garlic, allspice berries, juniper berries and fresh thyme.
3. Seal the bag and massage the duck legs through the bag till well combined with the spices.
4. Refrigerate to marinate for about 24 hours.
5. Set your oven to 200 degrees F.
6. Remove the duck legs from the marinade.
7. Rinse the duck legs and pat dry.
8. In the bottom of a baking dish, place the remaining marinade.
9. Place the duck legs, skin side down in a single layer.
10. In a small pan, melt the duck fat on low heat and place over the duck legs evenly.
11. With a lid, cover the baking dish.
12. Cook in the oven for about 6-7 hours.
13. Remove the duck legs from the fat and place in a resealable container.
14. Strain all of the solids from the remaining fat and discard them.
15. Place the fat over the duck in the container.
16. Seal and keep aside to come at room temperature.
17. After cooling, refrigerate for 2 months to cure.

NOODLES & Shrimp Asian Style

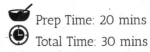

Prep Time: 20 mins
Total Time: 30 mins

Servings per Recipe: 6
Calories   322 kcal
Fat   6.3 g
Carbohydrates   49 g
Protein   15.1 g
Cholesterol   83 mg
Sodium   616 mg

Ingredients

1 lb. fresh Chinese egg noodles
2 tbsp olive oil
1/3 C. chopped onion
1 clove garlic, chopped
3/4 C. broccoli florets
1/2 C. chopped red bell pepper
2 C. cooked shrimp
1/2 C. sliced water chestnuts, drained
1/2 C. baby corn, drained
1/2 C. canned sliced bamboo shoots, drained
3 tbsp oyster sauce
1 tbsp red pepper flakes, or to taste

Directions

1. In a large pan of lightly salted boiling water, cook the egg noodles for about 1-2 minutes.
2. Drain them well and keep everything aside.
3. In a large skillet, heat the oil on medium-high heat, sauté the onion and garlic for about 1 minute.
4. Stir in the bell pepper and broccoli and stir fry everything for about 3 minutes.
5. Stir in the remaining ingredients and cook for about 3 more minutes.
6. Serve the noodles with a topping of the veggie mixture.

Chicken and Onion Egg Noodle Dump Dinner

Prep Time: 30 mins
Total Time: 8 hrs 30 mins

Servings per Recipe: 6
Calories   311 kcal
Fat   3.5 g
Carbohydrates   42g
Protein   26.4 g
Cholesterol   93 mg
Sodium   81 mg

Ingredients

4 skinless, boneless chicken breast halves
6 C. water
1 onion, chopped
2 stalks celery, chopped
salt and pepper to taste
1 (12 oz.) package egg noodles

Directions

1. In a slow cooker, add all the ingredients except the noodles.
2. Set the slow cooker on Low and cook, covered for about 6-8 hours.
3. Remove the chicken from the slow cooker and chop into bite-sized pieces.
4. Now, set the slow cooker on High.
5. Stir in the noodles and cook till the noodles are cooked through.
6. Stir in the chicken and serve.

HEARTY Chili Noodles Bake

Prep Time: 15 mins
Total Time: 50 mins

Servings per Recipe: 6
Calories 510 kcal
Fat 20 g
Carbohydrates 49 g
Protein 27.6 g
Cholesterol 111 mg
Sodium 1129 mg

Ingredients

- 1 (12 oz.) package wide egg noodles
- 1 lb. ground beef
- 1 onion, chopped
- 3 cloves garlic, minced
- 2 (15 oz.) cans tomato sauce
- 1 (8 oz.) can tomato sauce
- 15 fluid oz. water
- 1 C. beef broth
- 1 tbsp ground cumin
- 1 tsp dried oregano
- 1/2 tsp cayenne pepper
- 1 C. shredded sharp Cheddar cheese

Directions

1. Set your oven to 350 degrees F before doing anything else and grease a 14x9-inch baking dish.
2. In a large pan of lightly salted boiling water, cook the egg noodles for about 5 minutes, stirring occasionally.
3. Drain them well and keep everything aside.
4. Heat a large skillet on medium-high heat and cook the beef till browned completely.
5. Add the onion and garlic and stir fry them till the onion becomes tender.
6. Add the tomato sauce, broth, water, oregano, cumin and cayenne pepper and bring to a simmer.
7. Stir in the pasta and place the mixture into the prepared baking dish.
8. Top everything with the cheddar cheese and cook everything in the oven for about 20 minutes.

Comforting Noodle Soup

Prep Time: 10 mins
Total Time: 36 mins

Servings per Recipe: 4
Calories   536.3
Fat   12.8g
Cholesterol   115.7mg
Sodium   629.1mg
Carbohydrates   55.8g
Protein   51.1g

Ingredients

- 2 tsp olive oil or 2 tsp vegetable oil
- 2 leeks, cleaned and chopped
- 2 carrots, peeled and chopped
- 1 garlic clove, minced
- 1 stalk celery, chopped
- 3 - 4 C. cooked turkey, shredded
- 2 - 3 bay leaves
- 2 tsp dried thyme
- 1/2 tsp salt
- 1/4 tsp fresh ground black pepper
- 8 C. reduced-chicken broth
- 6 oz. egg noodles, uncooked
- 1 C. frozen green pea
- 2 tbsp fresh parsley leaves, chopped

Directions

1. In a large pan, heat the oil on medium heat, sauté the carrots, celery, leeks and garlic for about 4 minutes.
2. Stir in the turkey, thyme, bay leaves and black pepper.
3. Add the broth and bring to a boil.
4. Reduce the heat to medium-low and simmer, covered partially for about 10 minutes.
5. Uncover and again bring to a boil, then stir in the noodles.
6. Simmer for about 10 minutes.
7. Stir in the peas and simmer for about 1 minute.
8. Remove everything from the heat and discard the bay leaves.
9. Stir in the parsley and serve.

TASTIER
Noodles Bake

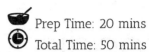
Prep Time: 20 mins
Total Time: 50 mins

Servings per Recipe: 4
Calories	740.5
Fat	49.5g
Cholesterol	195.3mg
Sodium	772.2mg
Carbohydrates	24.8g
Protein	47.5g

Ingredients

1 lb ground beef
1/2 C. green pepper
1/2 C. onion
1 tsp seasoning salt
1/8 tsp pepper
8 oz. tomato sauce with basic and garlic
4 -6 oz. egg noodles
1 C. cottage cheese
1 C. sour cream
1 1/2 C. shredded sharp cheddar cheese, divided
1/2 C. grated parmesan cheese

Directions

1. Set your oven to 350 degrees F before doing anything else and grease a casserole dish.
2. Heat a large skillet and cook the beef with the green pepper and onion till browned completely.
3. Stir in the tomato sauce and seasoning and simmer for about 5 minutes.
4. Meanwhile prepare the egg noodles according to the package's directions.
5. Drain well.
6. In a bowl, mix together the noodles, sour cream, cottage cheese and 1/2 C. of the cheddar cheese.
7. In the bottom of the prepared casserole dish, place half of the noodles mixture, followed by the beef mixture and the remaining noodle mixture.
8. Top everything with the remaining cheddar cheese and cook everything in the oven for about 20 minutes.
9. Sprinkle the dish with the Parmesan and cook everything in the oven for about 10 minutes.

Easy Homemade Noodles

🍲 Prep Time: 5 mins
🕐 Total Time: 25 mins

Servings per Recipe: 1
Calories   114.3
Fat   5.7g
Cholesterol   223.2mg
Sodium   90.3mg
Carbohydrates   7.0g
Protein   8.0g

Ingredients

6 eggs, beaten
1/2 C. water, room temperature
1/4 C. potato starch
salt

oil, for pan

Directions

1. In a bowl, mix together the potato starch and water.
2. Slowly, add the beaten eggs and salt, beating continuously till well combined.
3. Heat a lightly greased skillet on medium heat and add a thin layer of the egg mixture and cook till set.
4. Flip the side and immediately transfer onto a plate, uncooked side up.
5. Tightly roll it and cut everything into 1/4-inch circles.
6. Repeat with the remaining egg mixture.
7. These noodles can be used in any soup.

FAMILY-FRIENDLY
Noodle Casserole

Prep Time: 30 mins
Total Time: 1 hr 20 mins

Servings per Recipe: 9
Calories   524 kcal
Fat   30.9 g
Carbohydrates   42.2 g
Protein   21.8 g
Cholesterol   112 mg
Sodium   723 mg

Ingredients

- 1 (12 oz.) package egg noodles
- 2 tbsp olive oil
- 2 C. fresh sliced mushrooms
- 1/2 C. chopped green bell pepper
- 1 onion, chopped
- 2 cloves garlic, minced
- 1 lb. lean ground beef
- 1 (28 oz.) can crushed tomatoes
- 1 (6 oz.) can tomato paste
- 1/4 tsp chopped fresh parsley
- 2 tsp Italian seasoning
- 1 tbsp dried oregano
- 1/4 tsp cayenne pepper
- 1 tsp salt
- ground black pepper to taste
- 1 tsp white sugar
- 1 (8 oz.) package cream cheese
- 1 (8 oz.) container sour cream
- 1/2 C. chopped green onions
- 1/2 C. grated Parmesan cheese
- 1 pinch paprika

Directions

1. In a large pan of lightly salted boiling water, cook the egg noodles till desired doneness (about 5 mins).
2. Drain them well and keep everything aside.
3. In a large skillet, heat the oil on medium heat, sauté the bell pepper, mushrooms and onion for about 5 minutes.
4. Add the beef and cook till browned completely.
5. Drain the excess fat from the skillet.
6. Stir in the tomatoes, parsley, tomato paste, Italian seasoning, oregano, cayenne pepper, salt and black pepper and simmer, covered for about 30 minutes, , stirring occasionally.
7. Set your oven to 325 degrees F and grease a large casserole dish.
8. In a bowl, mix together the sour cream, cream cheese, 1/4 C. of the Parmesan and green onion.
9. Place the cooked noodles in the bottom of the casserole dish evenly, followed by the tomato mixture, cream cheese mixture and top the mix with the remaining Parmesan and paprika.
10. Cook everything in the oven for about 45 minutes.

Egg Rolls

Prep Time: 15 mins
Total Time: 35 mins

Servings per Recipe: 4
Calories   233.3
Fat   21.5g
Cholesterol   59.2mg
Sodium   110.2mg
Carbohydrates   1.1g
Protein   8.7g

Ingredients

Vermicelli mung bean noodles
5 C. warm water
2 - 3 lb. ground beef
1 lb. shrimp
4 medium carrots
1/2 medium onion
1 tbsp black pepper
1 tbsp sugar
1 tsp salt
3 eggs, whites and yolks separated
egg roll wrap, thawed
3 C. vegetable oil

Directions

1. In a bowl of lukewarm water, soak the mung bean noodles until softened.
2. Drain the mung bean noodles completely.
3. In a large bowl, add the shrimp, beef, drained mung bean noodles, egg whites, onion, carrots, sugar, salt and black pepper and mix until well combined.
4. In another bowl, add the eggs yolks and beat well.
5. Carefully, separate egg roll wrapper and arrange onto a smooth surface.
6. Put about 2-3 tbsp of the meat mixture onto each wrapper.
7. Roll each wrapper according to package's directions.
8. Coat the edges with beaten egg yolks to seal the filling.
9. In a deep skillet, heat 3 C. of the oil over high heat.
10. Now, set the heat to medium.
11. Add the egg rolls in batches and fry for about 8 minutes per side.
12. With a slotted spoon, transfer the rolls onto a paper towel-lined plate to drain.
13. Enjoy warm.

HOT and Spicy Seafood Filets

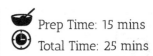

Prep Time: 15 mins
Total Time: 25 mins

Servings per Recipe: 6
Calories 94.6
Fat 7.0g
Cholesterol 0.0mg
Sodium 477.0mg
Carbohydrates 7.6g
Protein 1.3g

Ingredients

1 tbsp vegetable oil
fish (white fillet)
salt and pepper
2 tbsp vegetable oil
4 shallots, peeled and sliced
2 garlic cloves, chopped
1 - 2 Thai red chili pepper, cut in half
1 1/2 inches piece ginger, peeled and julienned
20 cherry tomatoes, cut in half
2 tbsp fish sauce
2 tbsp apple cider vinegar
6 tbsp water
2 tsp sugar
1 tsp paprika
1 tsp cornstarch
cilantro leaf

Directions

1. In a bowl, add the vinegar, fish sauce, water, cornstarch, sugar and paprika and mi until well combined.
2. Season the fish with the salt and black pepper evenly.
3. In a cast iron skillet, add 1 tbsp of the oil over medium heat and cook until heated through.
4. Add the fish and cook until half done from both sides.
5. Meanwhile, in a wok, add 2 tbsp of the oil and cook until heated through.
6. Add the shallots and stir fry for about 30 seconds.
7. Add the tomatoes and cook for about 4 minutes, mixing occasionally.
8. Add the vinegar mixture and cook for about 1 minute.
9. Transfer the fish onto a platter and top with the vegetable sauce mixture.
10. Enjoy with a garnishing of the cilantro.

Shrimp Wok

Prep Time: 15 mins
Total Time: 25 mins

Servings per Recipe: 2
Calories	305.8
Fat	15.1g
Cholesterol	142.8mg
Sodium	1411.5mg
Carbohydrates	25.0g
Protein	18.8g

Ingredients

- 1/2 C. water
- 1 tbsp oyster sauce
- 1 tbsp soy sauce
- 1 tbsp sugar
- 1 tbsp cornstarch
- 2 tbsp vegetable oil
- 2 garlic cloves, minced
- 1 onion, sliced
- 1/2 lb. shrimp, peeled and de-veined
- 2 large green tomatoes, sliced
- 1/4 tsp ground black pepper

Directions

1. In a bowl, add the sugar, cornstarch, soy sauce, oyster sauce and water and mix well.
2. Keep aside.
3. In a large wok, add the oil over high heat and cook until heated.
4. Add the shrimp, onion, green tomato and garlic and stir to combine.
5. Add the cornstarch mixture and stir to combine well.
6. Cook until desired doneness of shrimp, mixing frequently.
7. Stir in the pepper and enjoy hot.

SPRING ROLL Bowls

Prep Time: 15 mins
Total Time: 15 mins

Servings per Recipe: 4
Calories   21.0
Fat   0.0g
Cholesterol   0.0mg
Sodium   1060.3mg
Carbohydrates   4.8g
Protein   0.8g

Ingredients

chopped green onion
grated carrot
lettuce leaves, shredded
shrimp
grape tomatoes
diced cucumber
3 tbsp lime juice

3 tbsp fish sauce
1 tbsp sugar
1 tsp minced garlic
1/4 tsp minced hot green chili peppers
1 tbsp minced basil

Directions

1. In a serving bowl, add the shrimp and vegetables and toss well.
2. For the dressing: in another bowl, add the garlic, basil, fish sauce, lime juice, sugar and pepper and mix until sugar dissolves completely.
3. Place the dressing over the salad and toss to coat well.

How to Mince Chicken Chinese Style

Prep Time: 30 mins
Total Time: 1 hr

Servings per Recipe: 6
Calories   276.9
Fat   10.6g
Cholesterol   125.9mg
Sodium   1077.3mg
Carbohydrates   12.5g
Protein   31.7g

Ingredients

- 1/4 C. uncooked long grain white rice
- 2 lb. boneless skinless chicken thighs, cut into chunks
- 2 tbsp canola oil
- 4 garlic cloves, minced
- 2 tbsp minced fingerroot
- 2 small red chili peppers, seeded and chopped
- 4 green onions, chopped
- 1/4 C. fish sauce
- 1 tbsp shrimp paste
- 1 tbsp white sugar
- 3 tbsp chopped of mint
- 2 tbsp chopped basil
- 1/4 C. lime juice

Directions

1. Set your oven to 350 degrees F before doing anything else.
2. In the bottom of a baking sheet, place the rice evenly and cook in the oven for about 15 minutes.
3. Remove from the oven and keep aside to cool completely.
4. In a spice grinder, add the toasted rice and grind until a fine powder is formed.
5. Meanwhile, in a chopper, add the chicken thighs and pulse until ground.
6. In a skillet, add the canola oil over medium heat and cook until heated.
7. Add the green onions, fingerroot, garlic and chile peppers and stir fry for about 4 minutes.
8. Add the ground chicken and stir fry for about 4 minutes.
9. Add the sugar, shrimp paste and fish sauce and stir to combine.
10. Set the heat to medium-low and cook for about 6 minutes.
11. Stir in the herbs, ground rice and lime juice and remove from the heat.
12. Enjoy hot.

CHICKEN & Saucy Noodles

Prep Time: 15 mins
Total Time: 30 mins

Servings per Recipe: 4
Calories   437.4
Fat   14.7g
Cholesterol   84.2mg
Sodium   971.8mg
Carbohydrates   53.9g
Protein   23.1g

Ingredients

6 C. water
1/2 lb. egg noodles
1/2 C. water
1/2 tbsp cornstarch
1 tbsp fish sauce
1 tbsp soy sauce
1 tbsp sugar
2 tbsp vegetable oil
2 garlic cloves, minced
1/2 lb. boneless chicken breast, sliced
1/2 tsp salt
1/4 tsp ground black pepper
1 carrot, julienned
1 onion, sliced
1/2 lb. bean sprouts, washed and drained
3 green onions, chopped

Directions

1. In a pan, add 6 C. of the water and cook until boiling.
2. Add the noodles and cook until al dente, stirring occasionally.
3. Drain the noodles well and keep aside.
4. In a bowl, add the cornstarch, sugar, soy sauce, fish sauce, and 1/2 C. of the water and mix until well combined.
5. In a skillet, add the oil over high heat and cook until heated completely.
6. Add the chicken and garlic and cook until desired doneness of chicken.
7. Add the carrots, onion, salt and pepper and stir to combine.
8. Stir in the noodles and cook until heated completely.
9. Stir in the bean sprouts and cornstarch mixture and cook until desired thickness of sauce.
10. Remove from the heat and mix in the green onions.
11. Enjoy hot.

Vanilla Crusted Shrimp

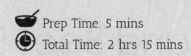

Prep Time: 5 mins
Total Time: 2 hrs 15 mins

Servings per Recipe: 6
Calories   920 kcal
Fat   81.4 g
Carbohydrates   35.8g
Protein   14.1 g
Cholesterol   117 mg
Sodium   225 mg

Ingredients

32 vanilla wafers, crushed
1 egg, beaten
3/4 C. water
1/3 C. apricot nectar
2 tsp cornstarch
1/4 C. packed brown sugar

3 tbsp apple cider vinegar
1 tbsp ketchup
2 C. vegetable oil
3/4 lb medium shrimp - peeled and deveined

Directions

1. Get a small bowl: Mix in it the vanilla wafers, egg, and water. Place the mix in the fridge for 1 h 30 min.
2. Get a small saucepan: Mix in it the nectar with cornstarch. Add the brown sugar, vinegar and ketchup.
3. Place the mix over medium heat and cook them while stirring all the time until it becomes thick to make the sauce. Place it aside.
4. Heat the oil in a large pot or deep fryer until it reaches 375 F. Coat the shrimp with the egg mix then cook it in the hot oil until it becomes golden brown.
5. Drain the shrimp and serve it with the ketchup sauce.
6. Enjoy.

TOFU and Beef Burgers

Prep Time: 25 mins
Total Time: 45 mins

Servings per Recipe: 6
Calories   307 kcal
Fat   18.1 g
Carbohydrates   8.9 g
Protein   25.5 g
Cholesterol   77 mg
Sodium   999 mg

Ingredients

1 (14 oz) package firm tofu
1 lb ground beef
1/2 C. sliced shiitake mushrooms
2 tbsp miso paste
1 egg, lightly beaten
1 tsp salt
1 tsp ground black pepper
1/4 tsp ground allspice
1/4 C. white vinegar
2 tbsp soy sauce
1 tsp garlic paste
1/4 tsp minced fresh ginger root
1 tbsp vegetable oil

Directions

1. Press the tofu and drain it. Cut it into 1/2 inch dices.
2. Get a large mixing bowl: Mix in it the tofu, ground beef, shiitake mushrooms, miso paste, egg, salt, pepper, and allspice. Shape the mix into 6 patties.
3. Get a small bowl: Mix in it the white vinegar, soy sauce, garlic paste, and ginger.
4. Place a large pan over medium heat. Heat the oil in it. Cook in it the patties for 3 min on each side.
5. Lower the heat and put on the lid. Cook the patties for 5 min. Drain them and place them aside.
6. Discard the grease from the pan. Add the white vinegar mix with the burger patties. Cook them on both sides until they become coated with the sauce.
7. Serve your burgers with your favorite toppings.
8. Enjoy.

A Uniquely Simple Cumber Soup

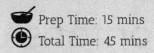
Prep Time: 15 mins
Total Time: 45 mins

Servings per Recipe: 4
Calories   67 kcal
Carbohydrates   6.8 g
Cholesterol   3 mg
Fat   4 g
Protein   1.7 g
Sodium   702 mg

Ingredients

1 tbsp vegetable oil
3 cucumbers, peeled and diced
1/2 C. chopped green onion
2 1/2 C. chicken broth

1 1/2 tbsps lemon juice
1 tsp white sugar
salt and ground black pepper to taste

Directions

1. Cook cucumber in hot olive oil for about 5 minutes before adding green onions and cooking for another five minutes.
2. Add chicken broth, sugar and lemon juice into it before bringing all this to boil.
3. Turn down the heat to low and cook for another 20 minutes before adding salt and black pepper according to your taste.
4. Serve.

MAPLE
Wontons

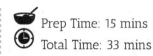 Prep Time: 15 mins
Total Time: 33 mins

Servings per Recipe: 1
Calories   45.1
Fat   0.1g
Cholesterol   0.7mg
Sodium   83.7mg
Carbohydrates   10.1g
Protein   0.9g

Ingredients

- 1 C. canned pumpkin
- 2 tbsp maple syrup
- 3 tbsp brown sugar
- 1 tsp allspice
- 16 packaged wonton wrappers
- granulated sugar
- ground cinnamon
- cooking spray

Directions

1. Set your oven to 400 degrees F before doing anything else.
2. In a bowl, add the pumpkin, allspice, brown sugar and maple syrup and mix until well combined.
3. Place about 1 tbsp of the pumpkin mixture in the center of each wonton wrapper.
4. With wet fingers, moisten the edges of each wrapper and then, fold over the filling in a triangle shape.
5. Now, with your fingers, press the edges to seal completely.
6. In the bottom of an ungreased baking sheet, arrange the wonton wrappers and spray with the cooking spray.
7. Dust the wontons with the cinnamon and granulated sugar and cook in the oven for about 16 minutes.
8. Carefully, flip the side and cook in the oven for about 2 minutes.
9. Remove from the oven and keep aside to cool.
10. Enjoy.

Silver Dragon Wonton Soup

Prep Time: 20 mins
Total Time: 28 mins

Servings per Recipe: 6
Calories   123.1
Fat   3.5g
Cholesterol   13.7mg
Sodium   973.7mg
Carbohydrates   11.2g
Protein   10.4g

Ingredients

2 green onions
1/4 lb. lean ground beef
1/4 C. chopped celery
1 tbsp chopped parsley
1/4 tsp salt
1 dash pepper
12 -18 wonton skins
6 C. chicken broth

1/2 C. spinach, shredded
1/4 C. shredded carrot

Directions

1. Remove the top from 1 green onion and cut into thin slices diagonally.
2. Reserve the slices for garnishing.
3. Then, cut the remaining green onions into small pieces.
4. In a bowl, add the ground beef, celery, chopped onion, parsley, salt and pepper and gently, stir to combine.
5. Place about 1 1/2 tbsp of the beef mixture in the center of each wonton square.
6. With wet fingers, moisten the edges of each wrapper and then, fold over the filling in a triangle shape.
7. Now, with your fingers, press the edges to seal completely.
8. In a pan, add the broth and cook until boiling.
9. Now, set the heat to medium.
10. Add the wontons in 2 batches and cook for about 4 minutes.
11. With a slotted spoon, transfer the wontons onto a plate and with a piece of foil, cover them to keep warm.
12. In hot broth, add the spinach, carrot and reserved green onion slices and stir to combine.
13. Divide the wontons into serving bowls and top with the hot broth mixture.
14. Enjoy hot.

CUCUMBER Wontons

Prep Time: 5 mins
Total Time: 17 mins

Servings per Recipe: 1
Calories 37.0
Fat 0.7g
Cholesterol 0.7mg
Sodium 46.3mg
Carbohydrates 6.8g
Protein 0.9g

Ingredients

cooking spray
24 wonton wrappers
1 mango, peeled, pitted and diced
1 cucumber, peeled, seeded and diced
1/2 red onion, diced
2 tbsp fresh lime juice
2 tbsp chopped cilantro
1 tbsp olive oil
1 pinch cayenne pepper

Directions

1. Set your oven to 350 degrees F before doing anything else and grease the C. of the mini muffin pans.
2. Arrange 1 wonton wrapper in each prepared muffin C. and press to fit in a C. shape.
3. cook in the oven for about 9-12 minutes.
4. Remove from the oven and keep aside to cool completely.
5. Meanwhile, in a bowl, add the remaining ingredients and mix until well combined.
6. Fill each wonton C. with the salsa .
7. Enjoy.

Artisanal Wonton Tins

🥣 Prep Time: 30 mins
🕐 Total Time: 1 hr

Servings per Recipe: 48
Calories   67.3
Fat   3.4g
Cholesterol   7.4mg
Sodium   141.5mg
Carbohydrates   6.5g
Protein   2.8g

Ingredients

- 1 C. freshly grated Parmesan cheese
- 1 C. mayonnaise
- 1/2 tsp onion powder
- 1/2 tsp garlic powder
- 2 C. shredded mozzarella cheese
- 1 (14 oz.) cans water-packed artichoke hearts, drained and chopped
- 1 (12 oz.) packages wonton wrappers

Directions

1. Set your oven to 350 degrees F before doing anything else.
2. In a bowl, add the mayonnaise, Parmesan cheese, garlic powder and onion powder and mix until blended nicely.
3. Add the artichoke pieces and mozzarella cheese and mix well.
4. With the cooking spray, spray one side of all wonton wrappers.
5. Place 1 wrapper into 1 of each mini muffin C. and press to fit in a C. shape.
6. Cook in the oven for about 5 minutes.
7. Remove from the oven and place 1 tbsp of the artichoke mixture in each C..
8. Cook in the oven for about 5-6 minutes.
9. Enjoy warm.

CABBAGE and Shrimp

Prep Time: 25 mins
Total Time: 35 mins

Servings per Recipe: 1
Calories 406 kcal
Fat 35.6 g
Carbohydrates 12.1g
Protein 12.3 g
Cholesterol 85 mg
Sodium 1017 mg

Ingredients

2 1/2 tbsps vegetable oil
1/4 C. water
1 C. shredded cabbage
1 tbsp minced garlic
8 large fresh shrimp, peeled and deveined
2 tsps crushed red pepper flakes
2 tbsps sliced onion
1 tbsp chopped fresh cilantro
1 tbsp soy sauce

Directions

1. Begin to stir fry your cabbage with 1 tbsp of water in 1 tbsp of oil for 1 mins.
2. Now place the cabbage to the side.
3. Add in 1.5 tbsp of oil to the pan and begin to stir fry your shrimp and garlic until the fish is fully cooked.
4. Now combine in the rest of the water, pepper, soy sauce, onion, and cilantro.
5. Let the mix fry for half a min then add in the cabbage and get everything hot again.
6. Enjoy.

Beef and Lettuce

Prep Time: 15 mins
Total Time: 1 hr

Servings per Recipe: 6
Calories 529 kcal
Carbohydrates 56.9 g
Cholesterol 69 mg
Fat 21 g
Protein 26.3 g
Sodium 1481 mg

Ingredients

1 cup uncooked long grain white rice
2 cups water
5 tsps white sugar
1 clove garlic, minced
1/4 cup fish sauce
5 tbsps water
1 1/2 tbsps chili sauce
1 lemon, juiced
2 tbsps vegetable oil
3 cloves garlic, minced
1 pound ground beef
1 tbsp ground cumin
1 (28 ounce) can canned diced tomatoes
2 cups lettuce leaves, torn into 1/2 inch wide strips

Directions

1. Bring the water containing rice to boil before turning down the heat to low and cooking for 25 minutes.
2. Add mashed sugar and garlic to the mixture of chili sauce, fish sauce, lemon juice and water in a medium sized bowl.
3. Cook garlic in hot oil before adding beef and cumin, and cooking all this until you see that it is brown.
4. Now add half of that fish sauce mixture and tomatoes into the pan, and after turning down the heat to low, cook all this for twenty more minutes.
5. Add lettuce into this beef mixture before serving this over the cooked rice along with that remaining fish sauce.

PIEROGIES
Re-Imagined

Prep Time: 15 mins
Total Time: 45 mins

Servings per Recipe: 4
Calories   473 kcal
Carbohydrates   48.6 g
Cholesterol   20 mg
Fat   28.6 g
Protein   9.2 g
Sodium   964 mg

Ingredients

6 tbsps vegetable oil
1 medium head cabbage, coarsely chopped
1 onion, chopped
1 tsp salt
1/4 tsp ground black pepper
1/4 tsp garlic powder
1 (16 ounce) package frozen pierogies
2 tbsps butter
2 tomatoes, seeded and diced

Directions

1. Cook cabbage, garlic, onion, ground black pepper and salt in hot oil for about 30 minutes.
2. Put pierogies into boiling salted water and cook for about 10 minutes and add some butter after draining.
3. Add tomatoes into the cabbage mixture just before it is done and add pierogies as well.
4. Mix it thoroughly and continue to cook until the pierogies are done.
5. Serve.

Turkey Bacon Dumplings

Prep Time: 10 mins
Total Time: 30 mins

Servings per Recipe: 8
Calories   184 kcal
Carbohydrates   27.4 g
Cholesterol   52 mg
Fat   5.1 g
Protein   6.4 g
Sodium   499 mg

Ingredients

2 slices turkey bacon
2 cups all-purpose flour
1 pinch salt
1 1/2 tbsps baking powder
1 tsp dried parsley
ground black pepper to taste

2 eggs
1/4 cup milk
1 quart vegetable broth

Directions

1. Cook bacon in a skillet until brown before setting aside after crumbling.
2. Combine flour, baking powder, pepper, salt and parsley in a bowl.
3. Whisk eggs and milk together in a cup, making sure that half of the cup is filled.
4. Now add this mixture and the bacon drippings into the flour, and mix thoroughly, while adding more milk if the mixture is too dry, form dumplings.
5. Now add crumbled bacon into it before cooking this in the hot broth over medium heat for about 12 minutes, while making it sure that the saucepan is covered in this time.

MEAT
Kabobs

Prep Time: 15 mins
Total Time: 2 hrs 20 mins

Servings per Recipe: 4
Calories	200 kcal
Carbohydrates	6.5 g
Cholesterol	69 mg
Fat	5.4 g
Protein	25.1 g
Sodium	419 mg

Ingredients

- 1 onion, chopped
- 1 clove garlic, minced
- 1 1/2 tbsps soy sauce
- 1 tsp ground coriander
- 1 tsp ground cumin
- 1 tsp sambal oelek (sriracha sauce)
- 1/2 cup beef broth
- 1 1/2 tbsps water
- 1 lemon grass, bruised, and cut into 1 inch pieces
- 1 pound sirloin steak, cut into 1-inch cubes

Directions

1. At first you need to set a grill or grilling plate to medium heat and put some oil before starting anything else.
2. Blend onion, garlic, coriander, cumin, soy sauce, sambal oelek, broth and water in a blender until smooth before adding lemon grass and coating beef with this marinade.
3. Wrap it up with a plastic bag and refrigerate it for at least two hours.
4. Thread these beef pieces onto the skewers.
5. Cook this on the preheated grill for about 5 minutes each side or until tender.
6. NOTE: If using a grilling plate please adjust the cooking time of the meat, to make sure that everything is cooked fully through.

Spicy Eggs

Prep Time: 15 mins
Total Time: 35 mins

Servings per Recipe: 6
Calories   237 kcal
Carbohydrates   13.1 g
Cholesterol   201 mg
Fat   17.3 g
Protein   9.1 g
Sodium   115 mg

Ingredients

1 cup vegetable oil for frying
6 hard-boiled eggs, shells removed
6 red chili peppers, seeded and chopped
4 cloves garlic
4 medium shallots
2 tomatoes, quartered
1 tsp shrimp paste
1 1/2 tbsps peanut oil
1 tbsp vegetable oil
1 tsp white vinegar
1 tsp white sugar
salt and pepper to taste

Directions

1. Deep fry eggs in a pan for about seven minutes over medium heat or until golden brown in color.
2. Put chili peppers, shallots, garlic, tomatoes, and shrimp in a blender until you see that the required smoothness is achieved.
3. Cook chili pepper mixture in hot oil before adding vinegar, pepper, sugar, fried eggs and salt into a mixture.
4. Turn down the heat to medium and cook it for about 5 minutes, while turning it frequently.
5. Serve.

SHRIMP
Veggie Salad

Prep Time: 20 mins
Total Time: 45 mins

Servings per Recipe: 4
Calories   250 kcal
Carbohydrates   18.7 g
Cholesterol   106 mg
Fat   11.9 g
Protein   18.9 g
Sodium   819 mg

Ingredients

3 tbsps vegetable oil
4 cloves garlic, minced
1 onion, thinly sliced
10 ounces peeled and deveined medium shrimp (30 - 40 per pound)
1 head bok choy, chopped
1 1/2 cups chopped broccoli
1 1/2 cups chopped cauliflower
1 large carrot, thinly sliced at an angle
3 green onions, chopped
2/3 cup water
2 tbsps cornstarch
2 tbsps fish sauce
2 tbsps oyster sauce
1 tsp white sugar
1/2 tsp ground black pepper
salt to taste

Directions

1. Cook onion and garlic in hot oil for about five minutes before adding shrimp, broccoli, cauliflower, bok choy, carrot, water and green onion, and cook this for about 15 minutes or until you see that all the vegetables are tender.
2. Add a mixture of fish sauce and cornstarch, to the cap cai and also some oyster sauce, pepper and sugar.
3. Mix it thoroughly and add some salt according to your taste before serving.

Shrimp Spring Rolls

Prep Time: 45 mins
Total Time: 50 mins

Servings per Recipe: 8
Calories	82 kcal
Carbohydrates	15.8 g
Cholesterol	11 mg
Fat	0.7 g
Protein	3.3 g
Sodium	305 mg

Ingredients

- 2 ounces rice vermicelli
- 8 rice wrappers (8.5 inch diameter)
- 8 large cooked shrimp - peeled, deveined and cut in half
- 1 1/3 tbsps chopped fresh Thai basil
- 3 tbsps chopped fresh mint leaves
- 3 tbsps chopped fresh cilantro
- 2 leaves lettuce, chopped
- 4 tsps fish sauce
- 1/4 cup water
- 2 tbsps fresh lime juice
- 1 clove garlic, minced
- 2 tbsps white sugar
- 1/2 tsp garlic chili sauce
- 3 tbsps hoisin sauce

Directions

1. Cook rice vermicelli in boiling water for five minutes or until done and then drain.
2. Dip a rice wrapper in hot water for one second to soften it up before placing shrimp halves, basil, mint, vermicelli, cilantro and lettuce, and then roll this wrapper around these things.
3. Mix fish sauce, lime juice, garlic, water, sugar and chili sauce in a small bowl before adding hoisin sauce in a separate bowl.
4. Serve spring roll with these two sauces.

BROCCOLI
Ramen Salad

🥣 Prep Time: 15 mins
🕐 Total Time: 45 mins

Servings per Recipe: 6
Calories   280 kcal
Carbohydrates   53.6 g
Cholesterol   0 mg
Fat   4.4 g
Protein   10.4 g
Sodium   1351 mg

Ingredients

1 (16 ounce) package broccoli coleslaw mix
2 (3 ounce) packages chicken flavored ramen noodles
1 bunch green onions, chopped
1 cup sunflower seeds
1/2 cup white sugar
1/4 cup vegetable oil
1/3 cup cider vinegar

Directions

1. Coat a mixture of green onions, slaw and broken noodles with the mixture of sugar, ramen seasoning packets, oil and vinegar very thoroughly before refrigerating it for at least one hour.
2. Garnish with sunflower seeds before serving it.

Beef Ramen Stir-Fry

Prep Time: 10 mins
Total Time: 45 mins

Servings per Recipe: 6
Calories   297 kcal
Carbohydrates   7.4 g
Cholesterol   78 mg
Fat   18.4 g
Protein   23.6 g
Sodium   546 mg

Ingredients

1 pound ground beef, or to taste
16 slices pepperoni, or to taste
1 (14.5 ounce) can diced tomatoes
1 cup water
2 (3 ounce) packages beef-flavored ramen noodles
1 green bell peppers, cut into strips
1 cup shredded mozzarella cheese

Directions

1. Cook beef and pepperoni slices over high heat in a large skillet for about 7 minutes before adding tomatoes, content of seasoning packet content from ramen noodles and water into skillet containing beef.
2. After breaking ramen noodles into half, add this to the beef mixture along with green bell pepper and cook all this for about five minutes or until you see that noodles are soft.
3. Turn the heat off before adding mozzarella cheese and letting it melt down before serving.

RAMEN
for College

🍲 Prep Time: 5 mins
🕒 Total Time: 15 mins

Servings per Recipe: 1
Calories   500 kcal
Carbohydrates   66 g
Cholesterol   191 mg
Fat   19.2 g
Protein   17.4 g
Sodium   1796 mg

Ingredients

2 1/2 cups water
1 carrot, sliced
4 fresh mushrooms, sliced
1 (3 ounce) package ramen noodle pasta with flavor packet

1 egg, lightly beaten
1/4 cup milk (optional)

Directions

1. Cook carrots and mushrooms in boiling water for about seven minutes before adding noodles and flavoring packets, and cooking all this for three more minutes.
2. Pour egg into the mixture very slowly, while stirring continuously for thirty seconds to get the egg cooked.
3. Add some milk before serving.

Sesame Chili Beef

Prep Time: 15 mins
Total Time: 35 mins

Servings per Recipe: 4
Calories   657 kcal
Carbohydrates   56.8 g
Cholesterol   120 mg
Fat   34.7 g
Protein   29.9 g
Sodium   98 mg

Ingredients

- 1 tbsp vegetable oil
- 1 cup white sugar
- 2 pounds beef short ribs, cut into 1-inch pieces
- 2 green onions, cut in 2-inch lengths
- 1 green chili pepper, chopped
- 1 tsp ground black pepper
- 2 shallots, finely chopped
- 2 cloves garlic, minced
- salt to taste
- 1 tsp Asian (toasted) sesame oil
- 1 tbsp green onion, thinly sliced and separated into rings

Directions

1. Cook sugar in hot oil in a skillet until you see that it is turning brown in color before adding beef, 2 green onions, black pepper, chili pepper, shallots, garlic, and salt, and mixing all this very thoroughly in the caramelized sugar.
2. After the beef turns golden brown; add sesame oil and vegetables into it before turning down the heat to low and cooking it for a few minutes.
3. When you see that juices have been absorbed then turn up the heat to high and cook all this for five minutes or until you see that the sauce is thick enough.
4. Garnish this with some green onion rings.
5. Serve

FISH SAUCE, Garlic Beef

Prep Time: 10 mins
Total Time: 2 hrs 30 mins

Servings per Recipe: 4
Calories   288 kcal
Carbohydrates   4.4 g
Cholesterol   85 mg
Fat   16.4 g
Protein   29.5
Sodium   713 mg

Ingredients

4 pounds beef shoulder, cut into cubes
1 tsp salt
1 tsp ground black pepper
1/4 cup olive oil
2 cloves garlic, minced
2 tbsps brown sugar
2 tbsps soy sauce
1 tbsp fish sauce
1 tsp Chinese five-spice powder

Directions

1. Cook garlic and beef that is seasoned with salt and pepper in hot oil for about ten minutes or until you see that beef is browned.
2. Now add brown sugar, five-spice powder, soy sauce and fish sauce into the beef before turning down the heat to low and cooking it for 2 full hours or until you see that beef is tender.
3. Serve.

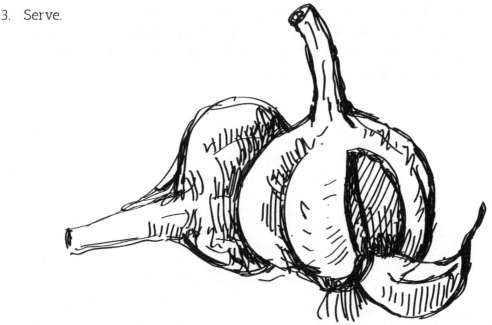

Peking Fried Rice

Prep Time: 15 mins
Total Time: 40 mins

Servings per Recipe: 4
Calories   375 kcal
Fat   15.7 g
Carbohydrates   35.8 g
Protein   20.7 g
Cholesterol   144 mg
Sodium   528 mg

Ingredients

- 1 C. chopped Chinese roast duck meat, skin and fat separated and set aside
- 1/2 C. thinly sliced Chinese barbecued beef
- 6 green onions, thinly sliced
- 2 tbsp soy sauce
- 2 eggs, beaten
- 3 C. cooked long-grain rice
- salt and pepper, to taste

Directions

1. In a large skillet, add the duck skin and fat on medium heat and cook for about 10 minutes.
2. Increase the heat to medium-high and stir in the duck meat, beef, half of the green onions, and the soy sauce.
3. Cook for about 5 minutes, stirring continuously.
4. Add the rice and cook for about 5 minutes, tossing occasionally.
5. Make a wide well in the middle of the rice, exposing the bottom of the pan.
6. Add the beaten eggs in the well and cook till scrambled.
7. Stir the scrambled eggs into the rice mixture and cook for about 5 minutes.
8. Stir in the salt and pepper and serve.

CHICKEN Stir Fry with Noodles

Prep Time: 15 mins
Total Time: 35 mins

Servings per Recipe: 4
Calories   445 kcal
Fat   11.4 g
Carbohydrates   60.6 g
Protein   18 g
Cholesterol   33 mg
Sodium   1415 mg

Ingredients

1 large skinless, boneless chicken breast, cut in bite-sized pieces
1 pinch garlic powder, or to taste
1 pinch onion powder, or to taste
freshly ground black pepper to taste
1 (8 oz) package dried rice noodles
4 C. hot water, or as needed
3 tbsp vegetable oil, divided
4 cloves garlic, minced
1 onion, chopped
1 green bell pepper, chopped
1/2 C. chicken broth, or to taste
1/4 C. soy sauce, or to taste
2 tbsp teriyaki sauce, or to taste
1 (6 oz) can sweet baby corn, drained
3 green onions, chopped

Directions

1. Season the chicken with garlic powder, onion powder, and black pepper.
2. Fill a large bowl with hot water. Place in it the noodles and let the soak for 12 min. Remove it from the water and slice it in half.
3. Place a large pan over medium heat. Heat 1 1/2 tbsp of oil in it. Add the garlic and cook it for 1 min 30 sec.
4. Stir in the bell pepper with onion and cook them for 6 min while stirring all the time. Stir in the remaining oil.
5. Add the chicken and cook them for 8 min while stirring them often. Add the broth, soy sauce, and teriyaki sauce. Cook the stir fry for 4 min.
6. Stir in the baby corn and green onions with rice and noodles. Cook them for 4 min.
7. Serve your stir fry warm.
8. Enjoy.

Garlicky Bok Choy

Prep Time: 10 mins
Total Time: 20 mins

Servings per Recipe: 3
Calories   223 kcal
Fat   10.2 g
Carbohydrates   25.1g
Protein   15.8 g
Cholesterol   27 mg
Sodium   1898 mg

Ingredients

2 tbsp butter
1/4 C. minced garlic
2 (14 oz.) cans chicken broth
6 heads baby bok choy, trimmed
salt to taste
ground black pepper to taste

Directions

1. In a pan, melt the butter on medium heat and sauté the garlic for about 5 minutes.
2. Add the chicken broth, baby bok choy and bring to a boil.
3. Reduce the heat and simmer for about 6 minutes and serve.

BOK CHOY
Skillet

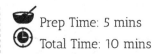

Prep Time: 5 mins
Total Time: 10 mins

Servings per Recipe: 2
Calories   95 kcal
Fat   7.3 g
Carbohydrates   6.1g
Protein   3.9 g
Cholesterol   0 mg
Sodium   163 mg

Ingredients

1 tbsp olive oil
1 clove garlic, minced
1 tsp minced fresh ginger root
5 heads baby bok choy, ends trimmed and leaves separated
2 tbsp water

Directions

1. In a large skillet, heat the oil on high heat and sauté the garlic and ginger for about 30 seconds.
2. Stir in the bok choy and water and cook, covered for about 2 minutes.

Bok Choy Appetizer

🥣 Prep Time: 10 mins
🕐 Total Time: 40 mins

Servings per Recipe: 4
Calories   149 kcal
Fat   9.2 g
Carbohydrates   4.9 g
Protein   2.2 g
Cholesterol   23 mg
Sodium   481 mg

Ingredients

- 3 tbsp butter
- 1 clove garlic, smashed
- 1 bay leaf
- 2 C. chicken stock
- 1 C. beef broth
- 1 lb. baby bok choy, trimmed and sliced in half lengthwise

Directions

1. In a large skillet, melt the butter on medium heat and sauté the garlic and bay leaf for about 5 minutes.
2. Stir in the chicken stock and beef broth, and bring to a full boil.
3. Cook for about 15 minutes, stirring occasionally.
4. Discard the bay leaf.
5. Place the bok choy halves, cut sides down into the sauce and reduce heat.
6. Simmer for about 10 minutes.
7. Pour the sauce over the bok choy and serve.

TUESDAY'S
Bok Choy Long Grain Rice

Prep Time: 10 mins
Total Time: 35 mins

Servings per Recipe: 4
Calories   191 kcal
Fat   1.2 g
Carbohydrates   39.7g
Protein   5.1 g
Cholesterol   0 mg
Sodium   210 mg

Ingredients

1 large head bok choy
1 1/2 C. cold water
1 C. long grain rice
1 tsp soy sauce
1 tsp chili-garlic sauce (such as sambal)
1/2 tsp sesame oil
1/4 tsp toasted sesame seeds

Directions

1. Separate the bok choy leaves from stems.
2. Cut the stems into 1-inch pieces and chop the leaves.
3. In a pan, mix together the water, rice and soy sauce and bring to a simmer.
4. Stir in the bok choy stems.
5. Reduce heat to low and simmer, covered for about 18 minutes.
6. Add the bok choy leaves, chili-garlic sauce and sesame oil and with a fork stir to combine.
7. Remove from the heat and keep aside, covered for about 5 minutes more.
8. With a fork, fluff the rice mixture.
9. Serve with a garnishing of the sesame seeds.

20 Min Vegetarian Bok Choy

Prep Time: 10 mins
Total Time: 20 mins

Servings per Recipe: 4
Calories	150 kcal
Fat	5.2 g
Carbohydrates	20.3g
Protein	13.7 g
Cholesterol	0 mg
Sodium	629 mg

Ingredients

- 1 tbsp vegetable oil
- 2 cloves garlic, crushed and chopped
- 8 heads baby bok choy, trimmed and cut into bite-size pieces
- salt to taste

Directions

1. In a large skillet, heat the oil on medium heat and sauté the garlic for about 1-2 minutes.
2. Stir in the bok choy and cook for about 5-8 minutes.
3. Sprinkle with the salt and serve.

GOURMET
Duck Rice

Prep Time: 2 hrs 30 mins
Total Time: 3 hrs 35 mins

Servings per Recipe: 3
Calories	946.5
Fat	34.5g
Cholesterol	402.7mg
Sodium	2590.2mg
Carbohydrates	96.3g
Protein	65.6g

Ingredients

1 lb boneless skinless duck breasts, in 1/2 inch cubes
4 tbsp soy sauce
2 tbsp hoisin sauce
3 cloves garlic, sliced

Brown Rice:
1 tbsp vegetable oil
2 cloves garlic, minced
2 C. chicken broth
1 C. brown rice

Fried Rice:
2 tbsp vegetable oil
6 green onions, white and 1/2 of green, sliced
1 C. Chinese pea pod, trimmed
1 small summer squash
1/2 yellow bell pepper, chopped
1 (10 oz.) cans stir-fry baby corn
1 tbsp vegetable oil
3 eggs, beaten
2 tbsp honey
1 tbsp soy sauce
2 tsp sesame oil
1/2 tsp garlic powder

Directions

1. In a plastic zipper bag, mix together the cubed duck breast with the soy sauce, hoisin sauce and 2 sliced garlic cloves.
2. Refrigerate to marinate for at least 2 hours.
3. For the brown rice in a large pan, heat the vegetable oil and sauté the 2 minced garlic cloves till golden.
4. Add the rice and sauté till aromatic.
5. Add the broth and bring to a boil.
6. Reduce the heat to low and simmer, covered for about 45 minutes.
7. Meanwhile, shred the yellow squash.
8. Drain the baby corn and slice the green onions.
9. Scramble eggs in 1 tbsp of the vegetable oil and keep aside.
10. Steam the pea pods and chopped bell pepper together for about 1 minute.
11. Immediately, plunge them into cold water after steaming.

12. In a large skillet, heat 2 tbsp of the vegetable oil on medium heat and cook the duck with the marinade and green onions for about 10 minutes.
13. Add the cooked rice and increase the heat a little.
14. Cook for about 10 minutes, stirring continuously.
15. Stir in the honey, soy sauce, sesame oil and garlic powder and cook for about 5 minutes.
16. Stir in the pea pods, peppers, shredded yellow squash, baby corn and scrambled eggs and cook for about 3-4 minutes.
17. Serve immediately.

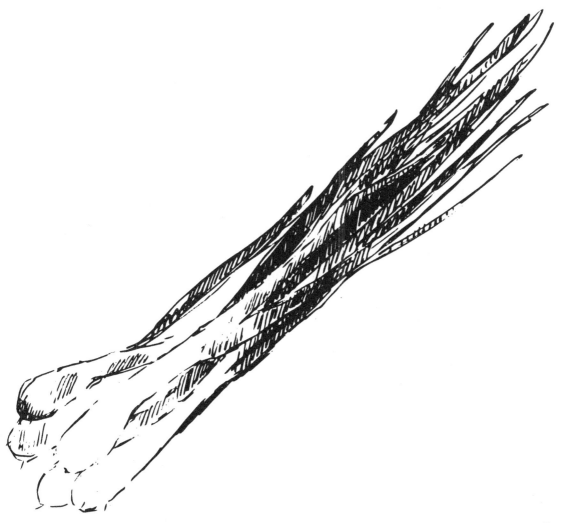

SUNDAY NIGHT
Duck

Prep Time: 10 mins
Total Time: 1 hr 30 mins

Servings per Recipe: 4
Calories	477 kcal
Fat	22.3 g
Carbohydrates	38.6g
Protein	30.3 g
Cholesterol	123 mg
Sodium	1069 mg

Ingredients

1 (4 lb.) whole duck
salt and pepper to taste
1 tsp poultry seasoning
1/2 tbsp butter
3 tbsp chopped onion
5 stalks celery, chopped
3 C. peeled, cored and chopped apple
3 C. cornbread crumbs
1 tbsp olive oil

Directions

1. Set your oven to 350 degrees F before doing anything else.
2. Rinse the duck and pat dry.
3. Rub the duck with the salt, pepper and poultry seasoning evenly.
4. In a small skillet, melt the butter on medium heat and sauté the onion and celery till tender.
5. In a medium bowl, mix together the onion mixture, apple and cornbread crumbs.
6. Stuff the duck cavity with the apple mixture and sew shut with kitchen twine.
7. Rub the outside of the duck lightly with olive oil and place in a shallow roasting pan.
8. Cook in the oven for about 60-80 minutes.

Chinese Styled Duck Rice

🥣 Prep Time: 15 mins
🕐 Total Time: 40 mins

Servings per Recipe: 4
Calories   375 kcal
Fat   15.7 g
Carbohydrates   35.8 g
Protein   20.7 g
Cholesterol   144 mg
Sodium   528 mg

Ingredients

1 C. chopped Chinese roast duck meat, skin and fat separated and set aside
1/2 C. thinly sliced barbecued beef
6 green onions, thinly sliced
2 tbsp soy sauce
2 eggs, beaten
3 C. cooked long-grain rice
salt and pepper to taste

Directions

1. Heat a large skillet on medium heat and cook the duck skin and fat for about 10 minutes.
2. Increase the heat to medium-high and stir in the duck meat, beef, half of the green onions and soy sauce.
3. Stir fry for about 5 minutes.
4. Add rice and toss together for about 5 minutes.
5. Make a wide well in the middle of the rice, exposing the bottom of the pan.
6. Add the beaten eggs and stir till the eggs are scrambled.
7. Stir the scrambled eggs into the rice along with the rest of the green onions.
8. Toss for about 5 minutes.
9. Season with the salt and pepper before serving.

HOMEMADE Egg Noodles

 Prep Time: 40 mins
Total Time: 3 hrs 50 mins

Servings per Recipe: 5
Calories	271 kcal
Fat	4.9 g
Carbohydrates	46.6 g
Protein	12.7 g
Cholesterol	112 mg
Sodium	294 mg

Ingredients

2 C. Durum wheat flour
1/2 tsp salt
1/4 tsp baking powder
3 eggs

water as needed

Directions

1. In a bowl, mix together the flour, baking powder and salt.
2. Add the eggs and the required amount of the water and mix till a dough forms.
3. With your hands, knead the dough till sticky.
4. Shape the dough into a ball and then cut it into quarters.
5. Place about 1/4 of the dough onto a floured surface and cut everything into 1/8-inch of thickness, then roll the dough from one end to the other.
6. Repeat with the remaining dough.
7. Cut each roll into 3/8-inch strips. (About 4-5-inch long)
8. Keep aside the noodles to dry for about 1-3 hours.
9. Cook these noodles in the boiling water till desired doneness.

Chinese Noodle Salad

Prep Time: 10 mins
Total Time: 20 mins

Servings per Recipe: 4
Calories	322.9
Fat	10.9 g
Cholesterol	43.2 mg
Sodium	505.0 mg
Carbohydrates	46.7 g
Protein	11.5 g

Ingredients

4 C. egg noodles, cooked
1 large avocado, cubed
1 C. imitation crabmeat, diced
1/2 C. water chestnut, chopped (canned)
1 red bell pepper, diced
1 tbsp horseradish cream

1/2 C. low-fat mayonnaise
1 tbsp fresh parsley, finely chopped
1 tbsp fresh chives, finely chopped
salt and pepper, to taste

Directions

1. In a large bowl, mix together the noodles, crabmeat, avocado, bell pepper and water chestnuts.
2. In another bowl, add the remaining ingredients and beat till well combined.
3. Pour the dressing over the salad and toss to coat well.

EGGY-WEGGY Noodle Bake

Prep Time: 15 mins
Total Time: 1 hr 25 mins

Servings per Recipe: 9
Calories 336 kcal
Fat 16.5 g
Carbohydrates 26.2g
Protein 20.9 g
Cholesterol 84 mg
Sodium 744 mg

Ingredients

1 tbsp olive oil
1 lb. extra lean ground beef
1/2 tsp ground dried thyme
1 (1.5 oz.) envelope spaghetti sauce seasoning mix
1 (6 oz.) can tomato paste
3 C. water
salt and black pepper to taste
1 (8 oz.) package egg noodles
1 (3 oz.) package cream cheese, softened
1 tbsp chopped fresh parsley
1/4 C. grated Parmesan cheese
1 (8 oz.) container sour cream
1 C. shredded mozzarella cheese, divided

Directions

1. In a large skillet, heat the oil on medium-high heat and stir fry the beef for about 5-7 minutes.
2. Drain the excess grease from the skillet.
3. Stir in the tomato paste, spaghetti sauce seasoning mix, thyme, salt, black pepper and water and bring to a boil.
4. Reduce heat to medium-low and simmer, covered for about 25 minutes, stirring occasionally.
5. Set your oven to 350 degrees F and grease a 13x9-inch baking dish.
6. Meanwhile in a large pan of lightly salted boiling water, cook the egg noodles for about 5 minutes.
7. Drain them well and keep everything aside.
8. In a bowl, add the cream cheese, Parmesan and parsley and mix till smooth.
9. Stir in the 3/4 of the shredded mozzarella cheese and sour cream.
10. In the bottom of the prepared baking dish, place half of the noodles, followed by the half of the beef mixture and half of the cream cheese mixture.
11. Repeat the layers once and top with the remaining mozzarella cheese.
12. Cook everything in the oven for about 35 minutes.

Oyster Sauce Beef Skewers

Prep Time: 15 mins
Total Time: 35 mins

Servings per Recipe: 4
Calories   1100.7
Fat   108.3g
Cholesterol   112.3mg
Sodium   649.8mg
Carbohydrates   22.3g
Protein   11.2g

Ingredients

- 1 lb. beef, tri-tip, sliced diagonally
- 1/4 C. lemongrass, chopped
- 1 tbsp lime zest, grated
- 1 head garlic, peeled
- 1 tsp turmeric
- 1 piece galangal, chopped
- 1/2 C. vegetable oil, divided
- 5 tbsp oyster sauce
- 3 tbsp sugar
- 1 1/2 tbsp paprika
- 1 kiwi, halved
- 8 bamboo skewers, soaked in water

Directions

1. In a blender, add the garlic, galangal, lemon grass, lime zest and turmeric and pulse until smooth.
2. Transfer the garlic mixture into a bowl.
3. Add 3 tbsp of the oil and stir to combine.
4. In a bowl, add kiwi flesh and with a fork, mash completely.
5. In a bowl, add 2 tbsp of the garlic mixture, kiwi puree, sugar, oyster sauce and paprika and mix until well combined.
6. Add the beef strips and coat with marinade generously.
7. With a plastic wrap, cover the bowl and marinate in fridge for about 4 hours.
8. Set your gas grill to medium heat and grease the grill grate.
9. Remove the beef strips from marinade and thread onto metal skewers.
10. Cook on the grill for about 6 minutes on both sides.
11. Enjoy hot.

CHICKEN
Pesto

Prep Time: 10 mins
Total Time: 30 mins

Servings per Recipe: 2
Calories   705.0
Fat   52.0g
Cholesterol   209.9mg
Sodium   1361.4mg
Carbohydrates   12.4g
Protein   46.3g

Ingredients

500 g chicken thighs, chopped
1 bunch basil leaves
4 hot chili peppers, chopped
1 handful peanuts
1 tbsp chopped garlic
1 tbsp fish sauce
1 tsp oyster sauce
1 tsp black sweet soy sauce
2 tbsp cooking oil
150 ml water

Directions

1. In a skillet, heat the oil and cook the chicken, chilies, garlic, fish sauce and water for about 10 minute.
2. Stir in the basil, peanuts, sweet soy sauce and oyster sauce and cook for about 2 minutes.
3. Enjoy hot.

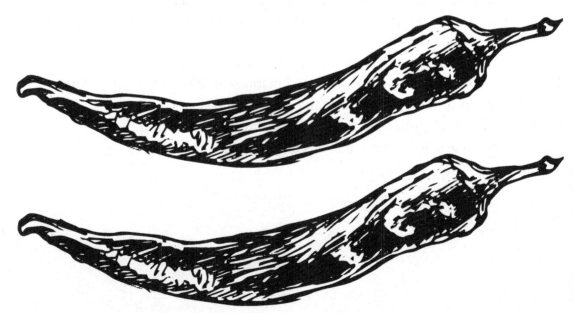

Chinese Backyard Chicken Thighs

Prep Time: 10 mins
Total Time: 35 mins

Servings per Recipe: 1
Calories	536.0
Fat	35.5g
Cholesterol	157.9mg
Sodium	2154.9mg
Carbohydrates	16.5g
Protein	36.6g

Ingredients

4 chicken thighs
1 tbsp vegetable oil
2 tbsp sugar
4 garlic cloves, crushed
4 tbsp soy sauce
black pepper

Directions

1. In a bowl, add the garlic, oil, soy sauce, sugar, salt and black pepper and mix until well combined.
2. Add the chicken and coat with the garlic mixture generously.
3. With a plastic wrap, cover the bowl and refrigerate for about 2 hours.
4. Set your grill for medium heat and grease the grill grate.
5. Remove the chicken from marinade and cook for about 25 minutes, flipping as required.
6. Enjoy hot.

SWEET and Sour Pie

Prep Time: 10 mins
Total Time: 13 mins

Servings per Recipe: 8
Calories   223.2
Fat   5.6g
Cholesterol   12.8mg
Sodium   174.4mg
Carbohydrates   36.6g
Protein   7.5g

Ingredients

3 C. nonfat yogurt, plain
4 oz. gingersnaps
2 tbsp unsalted butter, melted
1/3 C. light sour cream
1/4 C. granulated sugar
2 tsp tangerine zest, grated
1/2 tsp vanilla extract

2 tsp unflavored beef gelatin
1/4 C. tangerine juice concentrate, frozen, thawed
1 3/4 C. papayas, peeled, chopped
1 (11 oz.) cans mandarin oranges, well drained

Directions

1. Arrange a cheesecloth lined strainer over a bowl.
2. Place the yogurt into prepared strainer and cover it loosely.
3. Place the bowl in fridge until the yogurt reduces to 1 3/4 C.
4. In a blender, add the gingersnaps and pulse until fine crumbs like mixture is formed.
5. Add the melted butter and pulse until just blended.
6. In an 8-inch pie dish, place the crumb mixture and press in the bottom and up the sides evenly.
7. In a bowl, add the sour cream and yogurt cheese and beat until smooth.
8. Add the sugar, vanilla extract and tangerine zest and mix well.
9. In a pot, add the tangerine juice concentrate and sprinkle with the gelatin.
10. Place the pan over low heat and cook until the gelatin dissolves, stirring continuously.
11. Remove from the heat.
12. Add the gelatin mixture into the bowl of the yogurt cheese mixture and beat until well combined. Add 1 1/2 C. of the papaya and stir to combine.
13. Place the mixture over the prepared crust evenly.
14. Place the pie dish in fridge for about 8 hours or whole night.
15. Decorate the pie with the mandarin oranges.
16. Enjoy with a topping of the remaining chopped papaya.

Bean Sprouts Egg Rolls

Prep Time: 1 hr
Total Time: 1 hr 15 mins

Servings per Recipe: 1
Calories   77.2
Fat   1.9g
Cholesterol   9.2mg
Sodium   169.2mg
Carbohydrates   10.5g
Protein   3.9g

Ingredients

1 lb. ground beef
2 C. cabbage, shredded
1 C. bean sprouts
1 C. carrot, shredded
2 C. vermicelli rice noodles
4 garlic cloves, minced
1 yellow onion, chopped
1 tsp sugar
1/2 tsp salt
1 tsp chicken bouillon

3 tbsp oyster sauce
1 tbsp soy sauce
1/4 tsp black pepper
32 oz. egg roll wraps
oil
1 tbsp flour
3 tbsp water

Directions

1. In a bowl of the hot water, dip the rice noodles for about 13-15 minutes.
2. Drain the noodles well and then, cut into 2-inch long pieces.
3. In a bowl, add the rice noodle pieces, beef, cabbage, bean sprouts, carrot, onion, garlic, soy sauce, oyster sauce, chicken bouillon, sugar and salt and mix until well combined.
4. In another bowl, add the water and flour and stir until a paste is formed.
5. Roll the egg rolls according to package's directions.
6. Place about 1-2 tbsp of the beef mixture in the center of each wrapper.
7. Coat the edges with the flour mixture to seal the filling.
8. In a deep skillet, heat the oil and deep fry the wrappers in batches until golden brown from all sides.
9. With a slotted son, transfer the wrappers onto a paper towel-lined plate to drain.

CHICKEN and Jasmine Soup

Prep Time: 15 mins
Total Time: 30 mins

Servings per Recipe: 4
Calories   188.6
Fat   6.5g
Cholesterol   22.3mg
Sodium   1477.3mg
Carbohydrates   22.3g
Protein   9.7g

Ingredients

One 3-lb. rotisserie chicken
1 tbsp vegetable oil
2 tbsp minced ginger
2 garlic cloves, minced
4 C. chicken stock
1 C. water
3 tbsp Asian fish sauce
1 tsp honey
1 C. cooked jasmine rice
8 shelled and deveined medium shrimp, halved lengthwise
2 tbsp lime juice
1/4 C. chopped cilantro
2 tbsp chopped basil
1 Thai chile, sliced
lime wedge

Directions

1. Divide the chicken into breasts, thigh, legs and wings.
2. Then, cut each breast into 3 portions, through the bones crosswise.
3. Carefully, remove the thigh bones and cut each in half.
4. In a pot, add the oil over medium heat and cook until heated through.
5. Add the garlic and ginger and cook for about 2 minutes.
6. Add the rice, honey, fish sauce, stock and water and cook until boiling.
7. Stir in the chicken pieces and cook for about 6 minutes.
8. Stir in the shrimp and cook for about 1-2 minute.
9. Stir in the chile, basil, cilantro and lime juice and remove from the heat.
10. Enjoy hot alongside the lime wedges.

Curried Beef Fillets with Eggplant and Lime

Prep Time: 20 mins
Total Time: 40 mins

Servings per Recipe: 4
Calories   173.8
Fat   9.4g
Cholesterol   0.0mg
Sodium   718.9mg
Carbohydrates   22.9g
Protein   2.1g

Ingredients

- 1 oz. concentrated tamarind pulp
- 1/2 C. boiling water
- 1 lb. beef fillet, sliced
- 2 chilies, chopped
- 1 tbsp cilantro
- 1 tsp ground galangal
- 2 tsp ground lemongrass
- 2 tbsp vegetable oil
- 1 onion, chopped
- 2 garlic cloves, crushed
- 2 tbsp fish sauce
- 1 tsp sugar
- 2 oz. coconut milk
- 5 oz. eggplants, cubed
- 1 lime, rind grated and juiced

Directions

1. In a bowl, add the boiling water and tamarind pulp and stir to combine.
2. Keep aside for about 22 minutes.
3. In a blender, add the galangal, cilantro, chili and lemon grass and pulse until smooth.
4. In a skillet, add the oil and cook until heated.
5. Add onions and garlic and cook for about 3 minutes, stirring continuously.
6. Stir in the pureed mixture and cook for about 4 minutes, stirring continuously.
7. Add the beef and sear for about 4 minutes.
8. Add the sugar, coconut milk and fish sauce and stir to combine.
9. Through a strainer, strain the tamarind liquid into the skillet and stir to combine.
10. Cook for about 14 minutes.
11. Add the eggplant, lime peel and lime juice and cook for about 4 minutes.
12. Enjoy hot.

BARBECUE
Bacon Pancakes

Prep Time: 15 mins
Total Time: 45 mins

Servings per Recipe: 4
Calories 659 kcal
Fat 19.4 g
Carbohydrates 90.7g
Protein 29.3 g
Cholesterol 217 mg
Sodium 1531 mg

Ingredients

12 oz sliced turkey bacon
1 1/3 C. water
4 eggs
3 C. all-purpose flour
1 tsp salt
1 medium head cabbage, cored and sliced
2 tbsp minced pickled ginger
1/4 C. barbeque sauce

Directions

1. Place a large pan over medium heat. Cook in it the bacon slices until they become crisp. Drain it and place it aside.
2. Get a large mixing bowl: Whisk in it the eggs with water. Add the salt with flour. Mix them well. Stir in the ginger with cabbage.
3. Place a large skillet over medium heat then grease it with a cooking spray. Ladle about 1/4 of the batter into the hot skillet. Place 4 crisp bacon slices in the middle of the pancake.
4. Cook the pancake for 6 min. Flip it and cook it on the other side until it is done. Repeat the process with the rest of the batter.
5. Serve your pancakes with the tonkatsu sauce.
6. Enjoy.

Grilled Tuna Salad

🥣 Prep Time: 30 mins
🕐 Total Time: 1 hr 35 mins

Servings per Recipe: 2
Calories   252 kcal
Fat   19.3 g
Carbohydrates   9.3g
Protein   12.4 g
Cholesterol   19 mg
Sodium   207 mg

Ingredients

2 tbsp olive oil
1 1/2 tsp lime juice
1 1/2 tsp chopped fresh cilantro
1/2 tsp garlic, minced
1 tsp chopped fresh mint
1/2 tsp lemon juice
1/8 tsp salt
1 1/2 C. mixed baby salad greens
1/2 C. torn romaine lettuce
2 tbsp diced mango

1 1/2 tsp roasted peanuts
4 slices cucumber, quartered
2 tbsp crisp chow mein noodles
1 (3 oz) fresh ahi (yellowfin) tuna steak
1 pinch salt and ground black pepper to taste
1/4 avocado, sliced

Directions

1. Get a small bowl: Mix in it the olive oil, lime juice, cilantro, garlic, mint, lemon juice, and salt to make the salad dressing. Place it in the fridge for 1 h 30 min to 8 h.
2. Before you do anything preheat the grill and grease it.
3. Get a large serving bowl: Stir in it the salad greens, romaine lettuce, mango, peanuts, cucumber, and chow mein noodles.
4. Season the tuna steaks with some salt and pepper. Cook it on the grill for 2 to 4 min on each side.
5. Slice the tuna and place it over the salad. Drizzle the dressing on top then serve your salad.
6. Enjoy.

SPICY Lime Shrimp

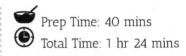

Prep Time: 40 mins
Total Time: 1 hr 24 mins

Servings per Recipe: 8
Calories 535 kcal
Fat 39.4 g
Carbohydrates 14.9 g
Protein 29.2 g
Cholesterol 173 mg
Sodium 648 mg

Ingredients

1/4 C. minced lemon grass (white part only)
1/4 C. minced fresh ginger root
2 tbsps minced garlic
1/4 tbsp chopped fresh cilantro
1 serrano chili pepper, minced
3/4 C. canola oil
2 lbs extra-large shrimp (16-20), peeled and deveined, tail left on
1/4 C. lime juice
1/4 C. apple cider vinegar
1/2 C. white vinegar
2 tbsps dark soy sauce
2 tbsps cold water
3 tbsps grated lime zest
1 tbsp minced fresh ginger root
2 tsps fish sauce
2 fresh Serrano chili, seeds removed
2 tsps minced garlic
1/2 C. smooth, unsalted peanut butter
1/4 C. peanut oil
2 tbsps chopped fresh mint
1 tbsp chopped fresh cilantro
1/4 C. unsalted roasted peanuts, chopped
Kosher salt to taste

Directions

1. Get a bowl, combine: 3/4 C. of peanut oil, lemon grass, 1 minced chili, 1/4 C. of ginger, cilantro, and garlic.
2. Stir in the shrimp to the mix and place a covering of plastic over everything.
3. Let the bowl sit for 40 mins.
4. At the same time begin to pulse the following in a food processor: water, lime juice, soy sauce, white vinegar, and apple cider vinegar.
5. Get the mix smooth then add in: peanut butter, lime zest, garlic, 1 tbsp ginger, 2 chili peppers, and fish sauce.
6. Continue pulsing until everything is smooth again.
7. Now set the processor to a low speed and gradually add in the peanut oil in an even stream.
8. Once the mix is creamy enter everything into a bowl. Then add in: pepper, mint, salt, cilantro, and chopped peanuts.
9. Cook your pieces of fish on the grill for 4 mins each side. When eating the shrimp dip the pieces in the peanut sauce. Enjoy.

Weeknight Ground Beef Wontons

Prep Time: 30 mins
Total Time: 40 mins

Servings per Recipe: 6
Calories   928.0
Fat   82.9g
Cholesterol   75.2mg
Sodium   468.2mg
Carbohydrates   31.0g
Protein   16.0g

Ingredients

- 1/2 lb. lean ground beef
- 1/4 C. yellow onion, grated
- 2 oz. cream cheese
- 1/4 C. cheddar cheese, shredded
- 1 large egg
- 2 tbsp dry breadcrumbs
- 2 tbsp taco seasoning
- 2 tbsp cilantro, minced
- 36 wonton wrappers
- 1 large egg white, beaten
- 2 C. canola oil

Directions

1. In a bowl, add the beef, 1 egg, breadcrumbs, cheddar cheese, cream cheese, onion, cilantro and taco seasoning and mix until well combined.
2. Place about 1 tsp of the beef mixture in the center of each wonton wrapper.
3. Coat the edges of wrappers with the beaten egg and fold them over the filling in a triangle shape.
4. Now, with your fingers, press the edges to seal completely.
5. In a deep skillet, add the oil and cook until its temperature reaches to 375 degrees F.
6. Add the wontons in batches and cook for about 2 minutes, from both sides.
7. With a slotted spoon, transfer the wontons onto a paper towel-lined plate to drain. Enjoy with a garnishing of the cilantro alongside the salsa.

MOZZARELLA Wonton Bites

Prep Time: 20 mins
Total Time: 38 mins

Servings per Recipe: 1
Calories   71.1
Fat   3.4g
Cholesterol   25.8mg
Sodium   164.8mg
Carbohydrates   6.1g
Protein   3.9g

Ingredients

24 square wonton wrappers
1 tbsp butter, melted
10 oz. shelled deveined and cooked medium shrimp
2 green onions, chopped
1/3 C. grated carrot
4 oz. cream cheese, softened
1 -2 cloves minced garlic
1/2-1 tsp Worcestershire sauce
1 C. grated mozzarella cheese

Directions

1. Set your oven to 350 degrees F before doing anything else and lightly grease C. of mini muffin pans.
2. Coat one side of each wonton wrapper with the butter evenly.
3. Place 1 wrapper into 1 of each prepared mini muffin C., buttered-side up and press to fit in a C. shape.
4. Cook in the oven for about 8 minutes.
5. Remove from the oven and keep aside.
6. Place 24 shrimp into a bowl and reserve them.
7. Chop the remaining shrimp finely and place into a second bowl.
8. In a third bowl, add the garlic, cream cheese and Worcestershire sauce and mix till well combined.
9. Add the chopped shrimp, mozzarella cheese, carrot and green onions and mix until well combined.
10. Place the shrimp mixture into each wonton C. evenly and top each with the reserved shrimp.
11. Enjoy.

Wontons Chips with Style

Prep Time: 5 mins
Total Time: 20 mins

Servings per Recipe: 6
Calories 688.4
Fat 7.7g
Cholesterol 19.2mg
Sodium 1450.6mg
Carbohydrates 130.6g
Protein 21.3g

Ingredients

Teriyaki Style
20 - 22 egg roll wraps
2 tbsp teriyaki sauce
2 tbsp honey
1 tbsp vegetable oil
Thai Style
20 - 22 egg roll wraps

1/2 tsp red chili paste
2 tbsp lime juice
1 tbsp vegetable oil

Directions

1. Set your oven to 400 degrees F before doing anything else and line a baking sheet with the parchment paper.
2. For the teriyaki chips; in a bowl add the honey, teriyaki sauce and peanut oil and beat until combined nicely.
3. Cut each egg roll wrapper into 3 portions.
4. Coat each side of each wrapper portion with the honey mixture.
5. In the bottom of the prepared baking sheet, arrange the wontons.
6. Cook in the oven for about 15 minutes.
7. Remove from the oven and transfer the baking sheet onto a wire rack to crisp.
8. For the Thai chips; in a bowl, add the oil, lime juice and curry paste and beat until blended nicely.
9. Coat each side of each wrapper portion with the curry paste mixture.
10. In the bottom of the prepared baking sheet, arrange the wontons.
11. Cook in the oven for about 15 minutes.
12. Remove from the oven and transfer the baking sheet onto a wire rack to crisp.
13. Enjoy.

HOW TO
Make Wonton Wraps

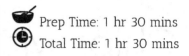

Prep Time: 1 hr 30 mins
Total Time: 1 hr 30 mins

Servings per Recipe: 1
Calories	981.5
Fat	7.2g
Cholesterol	186.0mg
Sodium	1242.3mg
Carbohydrates	191.1g
Protein	32.1g

Ingredients

2 C. all-purpose flour
1/2 tsp salt
1 egg
1/4 C. water
1/4 C. water
extra flour

Directions

1. In a bowl, add the flour and salt and mix well.
2. In another bowl, add the egg and 1/4 C. of water and gently, beat until well combined.
3. With your hands, create a well in the center of the flour mixture.
4. Add the egg mixture in the well and mix alongside the remaining water.
5. With your hands, knead the dough until a smooth dough forms.
6. Transfer the dough into a bowl.
7. With a damp cloth, cover the bowl and aside for about 1 hour.
8. Divide the dough into 4 equal sized portions.
9. Place one dough portion onto a generously floured surface and with a rolling pin, roll into a very thin circle.
10. Now, cut the dough into equal sized circles.
11. Repeat with the remaining dough portions.

Ginger Fish Patties

Prep Time: 15 mins
Total Time: 55 mins

Servings per Recipe: 6
Calories   319 kcal
Fat   5.6 g
Carbohydrates   32.1g
Protein   33.3 g
Cholesterol   82 mg
Sodium   596 mg

Ingredients

- 1 1/2 lbs fresh tuna steaks, minced
- 1/2 C. dry bread crumbs
- 1/4 C. finely chopped green onion
- 1/4 C. grated carrot
- 1 tbsp minced fresh ginger root
- 1 tbsp chopped fresh cilantro
- 1 tsp sesame oil
- 1 tbsp ketchup
- 1 tbsp lite soy sauce
- 1/2 tsp ground cumin
- 1/4 tsp salt
- 1/4 tsp black pepper
- 1 egg, beaten
- 6 hamburger buns
- 6 lettuce leaves - rinsed and dried
- 2 medium tomatoes, sliced

Directions

1. Get a bowl, combine: egg, tuna, pepper, bread crumbs, salt, green onions, cumin, carrots, soy sauce, ginger, ketchup, sesame oil, and cilantro.
2. Place a covering of plastic on the bowl and put everything in the fridge for 40 mins.
3. Now get the broiler of your oven hot before doing anything else.
4. Shape the mix into 6 burgers then put everything in a broiler pan.
5. Broil the patties for 5 mins each side.
6. Place your patties on some buns then top them with some tomato and lettuce.
7. Enjoy.

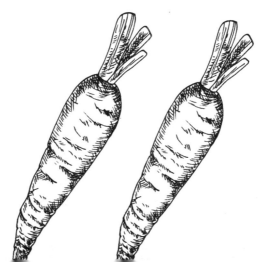

Made in the USA
Monee, IL
12 June 2025